Battleground Marlborough

RAMILLIES
1706

YEAR OF MIRACLES

Battleground series:

Stamford Bridge & Hastings by Peter Marren
Wars of the Roses - Wakefield / Towton by Philip A. Haigh
Wars of the Roses - Tewkesbury by Steven Goodchild
English Civil War - Naseby by Martin Marix Evans, Peter Burton and Michael Westaway
English Civil War - Marston Moor by David Clark
War of the Spanish Succession - Blenheim 1704 by James Falkner
War of the Spanish Succession - Ramillies 1706 by James Falkner
Napoleonic - Hougoumont by Julian Paget and Derek Saunders
Napoleonic - Waterloo by Andrew Uffindell and Michael Corum
Zulu War - Isandlwana by Ian Knight and Ian Castle
Zulu War - Rorkes Drift by Ian Knight and Ian Castle
Boer War - The Relief of Ladysmith by Lewis Childs
Boer War - The Siege of Ladysmith by Lewis Childs
Boer War - Kimberley by Lewis Childs

Mons by Jack Horsfall and Nigel Cave
Néry by Patrick Tackle
Walking the Salient by Paul Reed
Ypres - Sanctuary Wood and Hooge by Nigel Cave
Ypres - Hill 60 by Nigel Cave
Ypres - Messines Ridge by Peter Oldham
Ypres - Polygon Wood by Nigel Cave
Ypres - Passchendaele by Nigel Cave
Ypres - Airfields and Airmen by Mike O'Connor
Ypres - St Julien by Graham Keech
Walking the Somme by Paul Reed
Somme - Gommecourt by Nigel Cave
Somme - Serre by Jack Horsfall & Nigel Cave
Somme - Beaumont Hamel by Nigel Cave
Somme - Thiepval by Michael Stedman
Somme - La Boisselle by Michael Stedman
Somme - Fricourt by Michael Stedman
Somme - Carnoy-Montauban by Graham Maddocks
Somme - Pozieres by Graham Keech
Somme - Courcelette by Paul Reed
Somme - Boom Ravine by Trevor Pidgeon
Somme - Mametz Wood by Michael Renshaw
Somme - Delville Wood by Nigel Cave
Somme - Advance to Victory (North) 1918 by Michael Stedman
Somme - Flers by Trevor Pidgeon
Somme - Bazentin Ridge by Edward Hancock
Somme - Combles by Paul Reed
Somme - Beaucourt by Michael Renshaw
Somme - Redan Ridge by Michael Renshaw
Somme - Hamel by Peter Pedersen
Somme - Airfields and Airmen by Mike O'Connor
Airfields and Airmen of the Channel Coast by Mike O'Connor
In the Footsteps of the Red Baron by Mike O'Connor
Arras - Airfields and Airmen by Mikel O'Connor
Arras - Vimy Ridge by Nigel Cave
Arras - Gavrelle by Trevor Tasker and Kyle Tallett
Arras - Oppy Wood by David Bilton
Arras - Bullecourt by Graham Keech
Arras - Monchy le Preux by Colin Fox
Hindenburg Line by Peter Oldham
Hindenburg Line - Epehy by Bill Mitchinson
Hindenburg Line - Riqueval by Bill Mitchinson
Hindenburg Line - Villers-Plouich by Bill Mitchinson
Hindenburg Line - Cambrai Right Hook by Jack Horsfall & Nigel Cave
Hindenburg Line - Cambrai Flesquières by Jack Horsfall & Nigel Cave

Hindenburg Line - Saint Quentin by Helen McPhail and Philip Guest
Hindenburg Line - Bourlon Wood by Jack Horsfall & Nigel Cave
Cambrai - Airfields and Airmen by Mike O'Connor
Aubers Ridge by Edward Hancock
La Bassée - Neuve Chapelle by Geoffrey Bridger
Loos - Hohenzollern Redoubt by Andrew Rawson
Loos - Hill 70 by Andrew Rawson
Fromelles by Peter Pedersen
Accrington Pals Trail by William Turner
Poets at War: Wilfred Owen by Helen McPhail and Philip Guest
Poets at War: Edmund Blunden by Helen McPhail and Philip Guest
Poets at War: Graves & Sassoon by Helen McPhail and Philip Guest
Gallipoli by Nigel Steel
Gallipoli - Gully Ravine by Stephen Chambers
Gallipoli - Landings at Helles by Huw & Jill Rodge
Walking the Italian Front by Francis Mackay
Italy - Asiago by Francis Mackay
Verdun: Fort Douamont by Christina Holstein

Germans at Beaumont Hamel by Jack Sheldon
Germans at Thiepval by Jack Sheldon

SECOND WORLD WAR

Dunkirk by Patrick Wilson
Calais by Jon Cooksey
Boulogne by Jon Cooksey
Saint-Nazaire by James Dorrian
Normandy - Pegasus Bridge/Merville Battery by Carl Shilleto
Normandy - Utah Beach by Carl Shilleto
Normandy - Omaha Beach by Tim Kilvert-Jones
Normandy - Gold Beach by Christopher Dunphie & Garry Johnson
Normandy - Gold Beach Jig by Tim Saunders
Normandy - Juno Beach by Tim Saunders
Normandy - Sword Beach by Tim Kilvert-Jones
Normandy - Operation Bluecoat by Ian Daglish
Normandy - Operation Goodwood by Ian Daglish
Normandy - Epsom by Tim Saunders
Normandy - Hill 112 by Tim Saunders
Normandy - Mont Pinçon by Eric Hunt
Normandy - Cherbourg by Andrew Rawson
Das Reich – Drive to Normandy by Philip Vickers
Oradour by Philip Beck
Market Garden - Nijmegen by Tim Saunders
Market Garden - Hell's Highway by Tim Saunders
Market Garden - Arnhem, Oosterbeek by Frank Steer
Market Garden - Arnhem, The Bridge by Frank Steer
Market Garden - The Island by Tim Saunders
Normandy - Cherbourg by Andrew Rawson
US Rhine Crossing by Andrew Rawson
British Rhine Crossing – Operation Varsity by Tim Saunders
British Rhine Crossing – Operation Plunder by Tim Saunders
Battle of the Bulge - St Vith by Michael Tolhurst
Battle of the Bulge - Bastogne by Michael Tolhurst
Channel Islands by George Forty
Walcheren by Andrew Rawson
Remagen Bridge by Andrew Rawson
Cassino by Ian Blackwell
Crete - Operation 'Merkur' by Tim Saunders

With the continued expansion of the Battleground Series a **Battleground Series Club** has been formed to benefit the reader. The purpose of the Club is to keep members informed of new titles and to offer many other reader-benefits. Membership is free and by registering an interest you can help us predict print runs and thus assist us in maintaining the quality and prices at their present levels.

Please call the office on 01226 734555, or send your name and address along with a request for more information to:

Battleground Series Club Pen & Sword Books Ltd,
47 Church Street, Barnsley, South Yorkshire S70 2AS

Battleground Marlborough

RAMILLIES
1706

YEAR OF MIRACLES

James Falkner

Pen & Sword
MILITARY

First published in Great Britain in 2006 by
Pen & Sword Military
an imprint of
Pen & Sword Books Ltd
47 Church Street
Barnsley
South Yorkshire
S70 2AS

ISBN 1-84415-379-7
ISBN 978-1-84415-379-4

A CIP catalogue record for this book is
available from the British Library

Typeset in Century Old Style

Printed and bound in Great Britain by CPI UK

For a complete list of Pen & Sword titles, please contact
Pen & Sword Books Limited
47 Church Street, Barnsley, South Yorkshire, S70 2AS, England
E-mail: enquiries@pen-and-sword.co.uk
Website: www.pen-and-sword.co.uk

CONTENTS

Biographical Notes.. 6

Introduction.. 9

Chapter 1 **If We Lie Still, This Is All For Nothing**.................. 15

Chapter 2 **We May Have a Complete Victory**....................... 37

Chapter 3 **Almost as Murderous as the Rest** 57

Chapter 4 **Milord Marlborough Was Rid Over** 75

Chapter 5 **Save Yourselves If You Can** 87

Chapter 6 **More Like a Dream Than the Truth** 105

Chapter 7 **Walking Ramillies Battlefield: A Guide** 125

Bibliography 138

Index 142

BIOGRAPHICAL NOTES

Alègre, Yves, Marquis (1653–1733). French cavalry commander, taken prisoner at Elixheim. Marshal of France (1724).

Argyll, John Campbell, 2nd Duke, and Duke of Greenwich (1678–1743). Fought under Marlborough at Ramillies, Oudenarde and Malplaquet. A political opponent of the Duke, he was influential in the negotiations that led to the Union of England and Scotland in 1707. Commanded British forces in Spain in later campaigns. (See p. 76.)

Bringfield, Lieutenant Colonel James, Captain 1st Troop of Horse Guards (1695). Aide-de-camp to Marlborough, killed at Ramillies.

Cadogan, Lieutenant General William, 1st Earl (1665–1726). Marlborough's Irish Quartermaster General and chief of staff. Commanded Allied advanced guard at Ramillies and Oudenarde. Master General of the Ordnance on Marlborough's death (1722).

Churchill, General Charles (1656–1714). Younger brother of Marlborough and his General of Infantry at Ramillies. Commanded at the siege of Dendermonde and served in all Marlborough's major battles.

De La Colonie, Colonel Jean-Martin (*c.* 1672–1737). French dragoon officer on secondment to the Bavarian Army. Present at the Schellenberg, Ramillies, Oudenarde and Malplaquet. Author of informative memoirs. (See p. 62.)

Hay, Colonel Lord John. Commanded Hay's Dragoons (Scots Greys) at Schellenberg, Elixheim, Blenheim and Ramillies. Died of fever during siege of Menin, 1706.

Lumley, Lieutenant General Henry (1660–1722). Marlborough's British cavalry commander.

Maffei, Alessandro, Marquis de (1662–1730). Italian Lieutenant General of Infantry in the Bavarian service. Served at Schellenberg (1704) as second in command, and led a brigade in Ramillies village. Taken prisoner, he became involved in abortive negotiations for peace.

Marlborough, John Churchill, 1st Duke (1650–1722). Queen Anne's Captain General, 1702–1711.

Murray, Lieutenant General Robert (died 1719). Commanded Swiss brigade at Ramillies that sheltered Marlborough. Governor of Tournai (1709).

O'Brien (Clare), Charles, 5th Viscount. Exiled Irish Jacobite. Commander of Clare's Dragoons, killed in Ramillies village.

Orkney, Lord George Hamilton, 1st Earl (1666–1737). General of Infantry. Commanded British infantry in all Marlborough's major battles except Oudenarde. Became the first British Field Marshal in 1736.

Overkirk, Henry of Nassau, Count (1640–1708). Dutch Veldt Marshal. A close friend and supporter of Marlborough. Fought at Ramillies and Oudenarde, and died of strain during the siege of Lille.

Schulemberg, Matthias-Johan, Count (1661–1743). Hanoverian Lieutenant General, commanding Saxon infantry brigades at Ramillies.

Vendôme, Louis-Joseph de Bourbon, Duc de (died 1711). Descended from King Henry IV of France. Succeeded Villeroi as army commander in the Southern Netherlands after Ramillies.

Villeroi, François de Neufville, Duc de (1644–1730). Marshal of France. (See p. 39.)

Wittelsbach, Maximilien-Emmanuel, Elector of Bavaria (1679–1736). Governor General of the Spanish

Netherlands. Defeated at Blenheim (1704) and in conjunction with Villeroi at Ramillies. Attempted unsuccessfully to capture Brussels in 1708. Restored to his estates in 1714.

Württemberg, Prince Karl-Alexander, Duke (1661–1741). Major General of Horse, and commander of Danish troops at Blenheim, Elixheim, Ramillies, Oudenarde and Malplaquet.

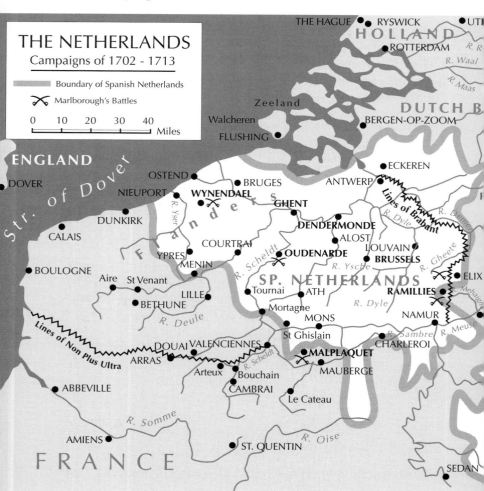

THE NETHERLANDS
Campaigns of 1702 - 1713

▨ Boundary of Spanish Netherlands
⚔ Marlborough's Battles

0 10 20 30 40
⊢——⊢——⊢——⊢——⊣ Miles

INTRODUCTION

THE BATTLE OF RAMILLIES, fought on Whit Sunday, 23 May 1706 during the War of the Spanish Succession, seemed to contemporary observers to bear all the marks of a miracle, no less – unexpected and astonishing, happening before their very eyes. The French and Bavarian army that took the field that fine day, commanded by François de Neufville, Marshal Villeroi, comprised 60,000 men, well trained and finely equipped. Their cavalry in particular was in fine fettle, included the bulk of the elite Maison du Roi cavalry, and would form a powerful striking force if used properly. On the day, by chance, and courtesy of good march discipline and rapidly drying roads, Villeroi and his troops got to the field of battle ahead of their opponents and settled nicely into a naturally strong defensive position. When the time came the Marshal's troops, on the whole, fought very well, in many cases with conspicuous valour.

Despite all this, and contrary to every expectation, Villeroi's army was utterly defeated in less than four hectic hours, shattered beyond hope of recovery by the 62,000 troops led by Queen Anne's Captain General, John Churchill, 1st Duke of Marlborough. Dazzled by the Duke's sudden and subtle moves and changes in emphasis, even while the fighting was in full and brutal progress, the French and Bavarian commanders simply lost control of the escalating battle, although, intriguingly, they did not realize that this was so until it was too late to attempt a remedy. Overwhelmed, caught in a tactical vice of enormous and unexpected force, their troops broke and ran en masse for safety. 'Save yourselves!' was the cry, and it seems that fully one-third of Villeroi's army ceased to exist, being casualties and prisoners, by the end of the day, and the demoralized remainder were hardly recognizable as effective soldiers still with their units. Those that rallied to their colours at all, and they were reduced enough in numbers, were in such a state of shock at the awful scale of their sudden and apparently inexplicable defeat, that, as one of their senior officers wrote to King Louis XIV the next day, 'The most dreadful thing of all is the terror that is in our troops.'

The Duke of Marlborough that day shattered the operational ability and effectiveness of the only army that the King of France had in the field in the Spanish Netherlands (today's Belgium). This was an army that had been substantially reinforced with cavalry just before the battle. There was nothing now to prevent Marlborough and his allies from pushing forward, as one later commentator so aptly wrote, 'as if the army had thrown its weight upon an unlatched door, and simply fallen through', and to conquer this rich and immensely important region, over which a long and expensive campaign of many months, possibly even years, might legitimately have been fought. As it was, in the wake of Ramillies, Marlborough took possession of the Spanish Netherlands in a lightning campaign of conquest lasting just a few short weeks, capturing such towns as Louvain, Brussels, Antwerp, Ostend, Ath, Oudenarde, and even the French fortress of Menin in the process. There was no French army in the field to oppose him, and the only thing that held the victor back in this triumphal progress was the lack of speed with which his supplies and siege guns could come forward across the appallingly bad roads of the time.

The political and military shape of Europe changed for ever that summer, and Louis XIV, who had lost the ability to win the war outright on Marlborough's victory at Blenheim in 1704, but had then recovered his position quite well in the following year, now lost the war itself at Ramillies in 1706. Of course, it remained to be seen whether he recognized this, and whether the partners of the Grand Alliance ranged against France, with all their narrow self-interest, contrasting ambitions and jealous bickering, would realize what a glittering prize lay before them. With careful negotiation, would they have the sense to offer the French

King a peace settlement that he could accept? Peace with honour and glory was almost certainly available after Ramillies, while peace through exhaustion might be the result of any prolonged delay.

The stunning victory at Ramillies is of enormous importance to Marlborough's reputation as a great commander. The success was not only achieved with verve and brilliance, overwhelming an opponent's army which was of nearly equal strength to his own and in a sound position, but it was achieved by the Duke without the assistance of his great friend and comrade, Prince Eugene of Savoy, with whom he worked to such good effect on other battlefields. The Prince at this time was campaigning in northern Italy, and during that same summer he would save Turin, and the Duchy of Savoy, for the Grand Alliance. Meanwhile, far away to the north, Ramillies proved in the starkest possible terms that Marlborough could rely entirely upon his own daring, calculation and skill, and did not depend at all upon the Prince for victory.

Frank Taylor, in his most useful study of Marlborough's campaigns, wrote approvingly in 1915 regarding his pre-wartime visit to Ramillies, of how unspoiled the battlefield had been, and he hoped that it would long remain so. He would not be disappointed today, for the battlefield, despite its quite close proximity to Brussels and Waterloo, is largely untouched by modern development and, thankfully, no one has thought fit to put a lion mound on it. The small villages round about are, of course, rather more substantial than in 1706, but the vast open plain to the south of Ramillies, on which a great swirling cavalry battle was fought, is still laid to wheat, and looks very much as it must have done on the day of battle. The marshy valley of the Petite Gheete to the north is drained now, but it still presents quite an obstacle to easy movement, just as it did to Marlborough's infantrymen on that long-ago Sunday afternoon in May, and it is easy to lose your footing when walking those slopes today. This really is a field of battle that no student of warfare should miss. It is a treat waiting in store, the scene of the most complete and sudden victory, brought about by subtle, brilliant tactics – tactics that were simple, almost obvious, but required the most skilful touch to bring them about and ensure fruition. Ramillies, as a masterpiece of generalship, is a battle that has no equal elsewhere.

Notes on Old and New Styles of Dating

In the early eighteenth century the Julian calendar (Old Style or O.S.) was still in use in the British Isles, whereas on the Continent the Gregorian calendar (New Style or N.S.) was used. This new system was ten days ahead of the old up to 1700, and eleven days ahead thereafter. As Britain adopted the Gregorian calendar later in the century, and almost all the narrative concerns events which took place on the Continent, I have used New Style dates throughout this book, unless indicated otherwise. At the time, the new year was not reckoned to start until Lady Day, 25 March, rather than 1 January as it does today. So, for example, 7 February 1706, as we would say now, was reckoned at the time to be still in the year 1705. Accordingly, care has to be taken when reading the dates on contemporary documents to make sure the right year is understood. However, as Marlborough did not cross to Holland to begin the campaign that led the armies to Ramillies until mid-April of 1706 (in other words, after the new year had commenced by the reckoning of the time) I will not add any further complication to the story.

There Are Soldiers, and Then There Are Soldiers

One of the confusing things about accounts of the wars at this time is the multiplicity of nationalities of the soldiers who took part. The French, Dutch and British (although the latter term was not really used until after the Union between England and Scotland in 1707) are all fairly easy to understand, but all these powers hired in large numbers of mercenary troops, often both sides recruiting from the same region, as with the Swiss who at Ramillies fought with the French (if they were Roman Catholic) and with the

Dutch (if Protestant). Considerable numbers of Scottish troops fought in the Dutch service, as well as with the Scots regiments in the service of Queen Anne. Some Irish regiments, composed of exiled Jacobites and Catholics, fought for France, whose Gendarmerie also included an English and a Scots company. Many small 'German' states provided excellent troops – again religion seemed to dictate which side they fought for. The Greder Allemende Régiment, for example, was amongst the best that France could put into the field, while two Saxon brigades took a prominent part in the bitter fighting for Ramillies village on behalf of their Dutch paymasters. The fine Prussian infantry were not on campaign trail yet, nor were the Hanoverians, but the Danish cavalry and infantry joined the Allied army on the march to battle, just in time to take a key part in the action. It was early in the campaign season, and quite a number of officers in both armies were still on leave and not with their units, this particularly being so with the Dutch. As the whole region had claims laid on it by the two competing Kings of Spain, loyalties were, quite understandably, a little mixed, but references to Spanish soldiers in the Ramillies campaign usually refer to Flemish and Walloon troops, whether in the service of Philip V or Charles III, not to those from the Iberian peninsula. These soldiers, Walloons and Flemings alike, despite the competing and confusing claims on their allegiance, were of uniformly good quality and were highly regarded by commanders on both sides.

The Wings of an Army

The right and left Wings of the armies in the early eighteenth century aided tactical flexibility, in many ways rather like modern army corps, except that unlike their latter-day counterpart the Wings would rarely operate independently. Each would be commanded by a general officer who would report, in turn, to the army commander. Care must be taken when reading the accounts of the battles though, as the terms 'right' and 'left' were descriptive only and did not always reflect their actual deployment; the left Wing was not always on the left flank, but the right Wing might well be found moving up on the left! Brigades at the time were formed on an ad hoc basis, with battalions grouped together depending on need, while divisions, or groups of brigades, were not in existence, although detachments from the main army of varying strengths were, from time to time, formed for a particular task. However, when the line of battle was formed, each 'line' would have its own commander, first line, second line, and so on. The first line, naturally, was regarded as the post of honour.

Spelling

The common usage of spelling has changed quite a lot over the years, and many villages in Belgium today bear a different name to that in use in 1706. I have tried to achieve consistency and clarity, particularly when contemporary accounts are used, so that the movements on the ground may be followed. The important hamlet of Offuz (as it is often named in accounts and on old maps) is now known as Offus.

Chapter 1

IF WE LIE STILL, THIS IS ALL FOR NOTHING

THE SICKLY KING CARLOS II of Spain (rather unsympathetically nicknamed 'the Sufferer') died on 1 November 1700, without children. No one wanted trouble over the issue, certainly not war, and plans had been made that a Bavarian prince, Joseph Ferdinand (son of the Elector, Maximilien-Emmanuel Wittelsbach), should have the throne when it became vacant, but that young man had died unexpectedly the previous year. As a result, the Second Partition Treaty, agreed in June 1699, set out that Archduke Charles of Austria should accede to the throne at the appropriate time, while French interests were to be catered for with territorial concessions elsewhere. The Austrian Emperor, Leopold I, had set aside his own claim in his youngest son's favour. Despite this practical solution to a tricky problem, French influence at the Court in Madrid led directly to the vacant throne being offered in the deceased King Carlos's will to the young Philippe, Duc d'Anjou, grandson of Louis XIV of France. Though aware that trouble might result, the Sun King reluctantly gave his consent to acceptance of the tempting offer. 'Gentlemen,' said he to his assembled courtiers, 'this is the King of Spain.' There was understandable and inevitable concern throughout Europe at the potential increase in Louis XIV's reach and power, once a French prince of the blood was on the throne in Madrid, liable to answer to his grandfather's bidding.

By the close of the seventeenth century, Spain was, it is true, financially lame and militarily almost impotent, but her vast empire stretched across not only most of the Iberian peninsula but also wide areas of Italy, the Mediterranean, the Philippines and the Americas. In addition, the rich Spanish (or Southern) Netherlands shared a long border with Holland, and this important region had, more than once, been the avenue by which Louis XIV, when in belligerent frame of mind, marched his armies to attack the Dutch. This concern over the future of the Spanish empire, and the extension of French influence, was made worse by a series of diplomatic miscalculations by Louis XIV (including the dreadful gaffe of recognizing the son of the exiled King James II as the rightful heir to the throne of England). The resulting outrage in London was severe and heartfelt, but this might have been smoothed over in time. Camille d'Hostun, the French ambassador to London, in particular, was very active. Of greater strategic concern was the French occupation of the Spanish Netherlands, where cherished Barrier Towns, guaranteed by treaty in the late 1690s and garrisoned by Dutch troops, were seized in February 1701. Louis XIV claimed to be protecting his grandson's possession, but actually he was spurred on to do so by Marshal Vauban, his engineer genius, who felt that the defence of France's northern border had insufficient depth to be really effective. This move forward offered the chance to improve things under a flimsy cloak of legality.

Although England and Holland had accepted the accomplished fact of Philippe d'Anjou (Philip V) having the throne in Madrid, with at least the appearance of good grace, these subsequent clumsy moves by Louis XIV led to the creation of a Grand Alliance, between England, Austria and Holland (Portugal and Savoy would join in due course). Their design was to limit this expansion to the power of France, by dividing the Spanish empire between French and Austrian interests, and (eventually, although it was not explicitly stated) to place the Archduke Charles (Charles III) on the Spanish throne instead of Philip.

Conflict on a wide scale came back to Europe in May

1702, when the Grand Alliance declared war on France and Spain. John Churchill, at that time Earl of Marlborough, was England's Captain General, and was soon appointed to be the commander of the Anglo-Dutch armies when in the field. His energetic campaigns to drive the French armies under Marshal Boufflers away from the southern borders of Holland were successful, and a number of important fortresses such as Liége, Venlo, Bonn and Huy were captured in the process. Still, Dutch caution frustrated his efforts to achieve an outright victory in the northern theatre of war during 1702 and 1703, while elsewhere the French war effort was doing rather well.

Marlborough, 'Victorious without slaughter' as he was hailed by the Dutch on a commemorative medallion, was made a duke by Queen Anne at the end of 1702, in recognition of these rather limited tactical successes.

On one of Marlborough's campaign marches the Captain General thought to attack the French in the area of the watershed between the Mehaigne and Petite Gheete rivers, near to a small village called Ramillies to the south-east of Brussels. The Dutch would not have it, as their field deputies, civilians who accompanied the army to ensure that the interests of the States-General were to the fore in the Duke's mind when

Queen Anne of Great Britain.

on campaign with their troops, insisted that the ridge-line was too narrow to be attacked with any real prospect of success. Dutch engineers had also surveyed the ground carefully, and declared it to be impracticable. Marlborough was at this time in no position to insist, as he could in 1706, but he took care to scout the ground thoroughly and store the information away for future use. Time would tell.

By 1704 Vienna had come under threat from France's ally, Maximilien-Emmanuel Wittelsbach, the Elector of Bavaria. The Duke of Marlborough's audacious campaign that summer took his troops away from the Low Countries, shaking off the cautious Dutch in the process, and confronted that devious nobleman, and the French Marshals Tallard and Marsin, in southern Germany. The bloody assault and destruction of Count d'Arco's corps at the Schellenberg hill in early July marked Marlborough as man to be reckoned with in open battle. Then, in August, the astonishing triumph over the French and Bavarian army at Blenheim on the banks of the Danube effectively put an end to any thoughts that Louis XIV may have cherished that he could decisively win the War of the Spanish Succession. No longer could France hope to exert its strength to knock out of the war any one of the main partners in the Grand Alliance – England, Holland or Austria – unless the wily old king could manage it in secret, by negotiation. This marked a strategic and irreversible shift in the war, assuming there was not some gross, inexplicable and catastrophic error by the Allies. Quite apart from the massive losses in men, horses and materiel suffered by the French at Blenheim, and the blow to French prestige amongst onlookers and wavering princelings elsewhere in Europe, the King's main ally, the Elector of Bavaria, was ruined and made a virtual fugitive. Louis XIV's other allies would not be at all encouraged. It did not follow, however, that his opponents, courtesy of the Duke's successes beside the Danube, could achieve a conclusive victory over France either; the immense resilience of the French King in the face of catastrophe, the strenuous efforts and, on the whole, skilful performances of his generals, enabled France to recover its poise to a significant degree by the early summer months of 1705. In short, Marlborough was not able to make the most of his victory beside the Danube.

Louis XIV of France. Crayon sketch, 1706. He urged Villeroi to go and fight Marlborough.

Emperor Leopold I died in May 1705, which unavoidably complicated things for the Grand Alliance, even though his successor, his eldest son Joseph, was a great admirer of the Duke of Marlborough. The Allied campaigns in northern Italy and in Spain failed to prosper very much, and the Dutch settled down to defend their borders and not do more for the time being. Meanwhile, the Duke's ambitious plans for a great campaign in the Moselle valley, with an advance aiming into the heart of France, was foiled both by the careful defensive moves of Marshal Villars, who took up a strong position at Sierck, and the reluctance of his allies, in particular the Margrave of Baden (who was, it must be admitted, very unwell at the time) to join him in the campaign at the agreed time and with the right number of soldiers. The overall effect was that in June Marlborough could deploy only about 30,000 troops, rather than the 90,000 he had planned for, and supplies were very short to feed those available (the Allied commissary officer in Coblenz having embezzled the funds and defected to the French to avoid retribution). The terrain was also poor, 'the terriblest country that can be imagined for the march of an army with cannon', and the weather was bad. In the meantime, to add to these local difficulties, in the Southern Netherlands Marshal Villeroi exerted pressure on the Dutch, by attacking and seizing the Allied-held town of Huy on the Meuse river, before threatening to move on Liége:

The Duke of Marlborough received an Account from the States [General] *of their Affairs in the Low Country, the loss of Huy, and the siege of Liége began, and the Threats that those two* [French] *generals made, that they would recover all the former Conquests of the Allies ... the States prayed his Grace that he would return with his Army from thence to the Maes* [Maas/Meuse].

Marlborough had no choice but to abandon the Moselle campaign, get his hungry army out from in front of Villars' stout defences, and march northwards at best speed to join the badly outnumbered Dutch commander, Veldt Marshal Henry of Nassau, Count Overkirk, who had gone into an entrenched camp near Maastricht for the time being. By employing a night march and rapid pace, Marlborough was able to disentangle himself from the French without his rearguard having to fight its way out. The Duke bitterly regretted that this potentially promising campaign, offering the chance to bypass the massive fortress belt along France's northern border, had to be let go. However, given the shortage of supplies, delayed appearance of Imperial reinforcements, bad weather, and Villars' astute use of the formidable terrain, the campaign was already, by the time Marlborough was summoned north, a dead letter, even before Marshal Villeroi took it upon himself to seize Huy and alarm the Dutch.

On 2 July 1705 Marlborough combined his forces with those of Overkirk, and the Allied army rapidly moved against Huy. Marshal Villeroi had already fallen back from an attempt to seize the citadel of Liége (having occupied the town) on news of Marlborough's approach, and he now went into camp at Tongres. Huy fell to Allied assault on 11 July ('Neither side had above twenty men killed and wounded', as one British officer remembered), and the French army then withdrew behind stout defensive lines, constructed over the previous eighteen months, known as

20

the Lines of Brabant. These works stretched in a great arc from Antwerp in the north, past Louvain, to Namur on the Meuse. From behind these defences Villeroi confidently expected to defy Marlborough and Overkirk with impunity. In their haste to get into their defences, the French under the Duke of Berwick abandoned the town of Leau, after blowing gaps in the walls.

Marlborough was anxious to regain the initiative, now that, very much against his will, he had resumed campaigning in the Spanish Netherlands, a region in which major success had eluded him in the past. In consultation with Overkirk, the Duke drew up an imaginative plan to trap the French commander. As Marlborough expected, the Dutch commander was cautious, aware that the States-General preferred to avoid open battle when they could. So, as Marlborough's chaplain, Francis Hare, shrewdly put it, the Dutch would 'follow him if he succeeded, to help him make his retreat if he miscarried, but not to share the danger with him.' Meanwhile, Villeroi had his field army well closed up, and was quite ready to shift this way and that, as the threat from his opponents appeared to be most acute, first in one direction and then the other. On the evening of 17 July, Overkirk began to march his Dutch corps southwards, using recently laid pontoon bridges over the Mehaigne river, as if to threaten the important French-held fortress of Namur on the Meuse. This movement was soon detected by the French scouts, as it was intended to be, and Villeroi took the bait; by nightfall he was marching his own main army southwards too, both to keep pace with the Allied advance and to cover Namur.

That same evening, Marlborough's troops were roused from their bivouacs at only a few hours' notice, and set to marching northwards, on a diverging course to Overkirk, heading for the section of defensive lines near the villages of Elixheim and Wanghe on the Petite Gheete stream. The Duke was quite deliberately dividing his forces, when in

The Lines of Brabant

Defensive lines of this sort in the early eighteenth century were not continuous defences in the modern sense of a trench system or a row of fortifications, but were more a series of obstacles, both natural (as with rivers or flooded meadows) and man-made (such as ditches, earth embankments and fortified farmhouses). These lines would be lightly garrisoned or patrolled by dragoons, and only manned in any force when a particular point was threatened by the approach of an enemy. The presence of a major part of the defenders' field army in a given vicinity would, naturally, deter any serious attempt to breach the lines, or incur heavy losses in the effort.

Great ingenuity was employed in making these defences formidable but simple to defend given their length, and engineers would carefully plot their course to take most advantage of the natural strength of local topography, for example following the course of a river or canal. The weak point in the Lines of Brabant, one that Marlborough was astute enough to recognize, was that there was a relatively narrow but perfectly usable watershed formed by high ground between the Petite Gheete and Mehaigne streams in the vicinity of the villages of Taviers and Ramillies. This was vital ground. Almost eerily, the French engineers recognized that any army occupying the position would naturally incline to throw forward the Wings to occupy the villages on either flank. Accordingly, any attacker approaching from the east would be able to switch troops from one side of the field to the other, cutting across the chord of the arc, thereby gaining an instant advantage over the defender, whose troops would have further to march when countering any such a movement. As a result, the lines had been pushed forward by French engineers nearer to Elixheim and Wanghe (close to the Williamite battlefield of Landen), in order to take advantage of the streams in that area, and avoid the inherent weakness of the Taviers-Ramillies-Offuz position. The lines of defence were, as a result, rather more exposed than elsewhere, and became the target for Marlborough's inspired attack in 1705. After the battle at Elixheim, Marlborough set his troops to work to level and spoil the lines in that area, and at the same time took the chance to thoroughly scout the local area, knowledge which he put to good use in May 1706.

very close proximity to his enemy, and this entailed some risk. However, Marlborough had assessed the character of his opponent well, and the speed of the Allied operation allowed little time for Marshal Villeroi to reflect on these developments, and form his own plan to interpose his army between the two separate and temporarily vulnerable Wings of the Allies. He instinctively swallowed the notion that Namur was the target of Marlborough's attack and took prompt action accordingly: 'This drew the Enemies main Force that way.' Villeroi was not so rash or neglectful, however, as to leave his left flank and rear areas entirely denuded of troops, and a powerful mixed corps of French and Bavarian cavalry and infantry remained in place, not far from Tirlemont, under the experienced command of the Marquis d'Alègre. Villeroi also left strict instructions that the troops were to keep on the alert.

Marlborough's marching columns, British, German and Danish troops, found the night heavy with mist and light rain, and the roads were bad. They made good time despite this, so that by dawn on 18 July the grenadiers and pioneers of the army were wading the Petite Gheete stream and breaking down the palisades of the Lines of Brabant in the area of the villages of Elixheim and Wanghe, near which was a fortified post. The few squadrons of French dragoons in the immediate area took themselves off to raise the alarm, and Marlborough's General of Infantry, George Hamilton, 1st Earl Orkney, wrote that 'though the passages were bad, people scrambled over them.' With the loss of hardly a man, Marlborough had breached the French lines of defence by about 7.30 that morning. However, with just thirty-eight cavalry squadrons and twenty battalions of infantry, under the immediate command of Count Noyelles, all intermingled together in the broken country beside the breach, laced through with muddy and sunken lanes leading up onto some higher ground, the leading Allied troops were hardly able to form up in some sort of proper order, when the inevitable counterattack came in. One Scottish soldier laconically remembered, 'When we were over on their side, they attacked us.'

The Marquis d'Alègre, an astute and skilful opponent, had fifty squadrons of French and Bavarian cavalry under his command, supported by Count Caraman, with twenty battalions of veteran Bavarian infantry. This was just an advance guard, and the two commanders might have done well to wait for their supports to come up and then deliver their stroke with full power behind it. However, they rightly saw that Marlborough would benefit by any delay, in getting his own army properly across the lines and so position his troops to meet any attack. They may also have suspected that the Allied intention was to combine with the Dutch troops, who having marched south were even now counter-marching northwards, crossing the bridges over Mehaigne river once again, to join the Duke at Elixheim. Of course, riders had been sent by d'Alègre, galloping off to alert Villeroi to the Allied breakthrough of the Lines, but it would take most of the morning for them to reach the Marshal with the news, and for the French field army to turn about in its tracks and, along with everyone else that day, hurry northwards to the beckoning sound of guns, gradually increasing in urgent volume as the early morning went on.

As it was, the French and Bavarians who confronted Marlborough at Elixheim were rather outnumbered by the Duke's corps, for many of the Bavarian squadrons, in particular, were badly under strength. As a result, it seems that Caraman and d'Alègre moved forward with only about 10,000 troops and ten guns to challenge Marlborough, who was able to deploy (albeit in very hurried and unsatisfactory formation) some 16,000 men supported by a six-gun battery. The blackened armour worn by the Bavarian cuirassiers as their leading squadrons shook out for action could be plainly seen in the morning light, and Marlborough, who could not have known for certain what a numerical advantage he actually had, was looking anxiously to the south for signs of Overkirk's leading Dutch regiments. He had thrown his troops over the obstacle in the most audacious style, with the loss of hardly a man; now the Duke had to hold onto the ground gained, long enough for the Dutch to join them.

The French and Bavarian troops came on in good order and a hard struggle broke out along the lanes and hedgerows in the area. The Bavarian infantry's coolly delivered volleys of musketry drove Noyelle's troops back a short way, but Marlborough hurried forward his reserves, and recovered his force's composure in the sabre-swinging cavalry battle that erupted in what little open ground there was available. Over the course of a two-hour battle, the superior numbers of Marlborough's force gradually began to tell, for all the dash and gallantry of the French and Bavarian attack. The Marquis d'Alègre was wounded, and taken away as captive by Lord John Hay. Without his guiding hand the ordering of the cavalry in the broken ground faltered, and many of the squadron commanders began to pull back into more open country, where they might recover their order. They were pursued by the Allied horsemen, also keen to get out of the restricting lanes, and what began as a limited tactical withdrawal by the French soon became a bit of a scramble. At this point, as Marlborough pressed the advantage onwards with his squadrons, he was confronted by a Bavarian horse grenadier, who aimed a mighty sword stroke at the Duke's head. The blow went wide and, the swing meeting no resistance, the Bavarian grenadier lost his balance in the saddle and fell to the ground, where the Duke's trumpeter leaped from his horse and killed him with his sword. 'Was it so?' Orkney asked Marlborough afterwards, 'and he said it was absolutely so.'

Count Caraman's infantry now found that their cavalry supports had melted away, but in a notably skilful manoeuvre, the Bavarian battalions formed themselves into a great square, with the grenadier companies taking up position at each corner, and began a steady and superbly well-ordered withdrawal to the west, heading for the river crossings over the Dyle river near to Tirlemont. Their musketry volleys deterred any close pursuit by the Allied infantry, and the perfect discipline of the square foiled all attempts by the Allied cavalry to interfere with Caraman's movement to the river. A British officer who watched the manoeuvre wrote admiringly, 'This shows what resolution and keeping good order can do.'

Despite this, Marlborough had won a notable victory. 'Half a battle', one observer rather disparagingly noted, 'as a half of each army were all that were involved.' Not only had the Duke burst through the vaunted Lines of Brabant with only light losses, but he had repulsed a very well-handled counterattack, inflicting hundreds of casualties and taking many prisoners, including the wounded French cavalry commander. Caraman's ten guns fell into Marlborough's hands also, and all this for the loss of little more than 200 killed and wounded. The regiments and squadrons with the Duke that day had all been with him in the Danube campaign, and the soldiers now crowded round his horse, shouting their cheers of triumph. 'See what a happy man he is', Orkney wrote; 'I believe this pleases him more than Höchstädt [Blenheim].'

The Duke did not pursue Caraman's infantry with as much vigour as he displayed on other occasions, and in part this had to do with the weariness of his own soldiers – they had marched all night and fought a hectic, if brief, battle in the morning. Also, Overkirk's Dutch troops were now arriving at the break in the Lines, but these men had also had a hard march, and the Veldt Marshal, usually so cooperative, was short-tempered, and asked that they be allowed to rest and eat something. The Dutch general, Slangenberg (so awkward and fractious on other occasions), was all fire and energy on this day, urging that a pursuit be mounted without delay: 'If we lie still, this is all for nothing.' Marlborough agreed with him, but would not overrule Overkirk, his good friend, and so, by 10 a.m. the Dutch troops had settled down to rest from their exertions. Although the Duke attracted some criticism for this apparent inaction, he had little option when faced with Overkirk's reluctance to

François de Neufville, Duc de Villeroi.

press on. He also had no way of knowing quite where the French main army was at this point in the mid-morning; Villeroi, having observed Caraman's masterly withdrawal from contact, was moving his troops back behind the comparative safety of the Dyle river, in such haste that he abandoned some of his artillery on the way, but Marlborough would not learn this for certain until later in the day. A British officer who was present wrote, 'The Duke really neither did nor indeed could at that time know how near the Elector and M. Villeroi was with their whole army.' As it was, the moment to move in hard against the exposed flank of the marching French army had passed.

Suitably rested and refreshed, the Allied troops pressed forward to the line of the Dyle the following day, 19 July. Tirlemont had already been occupied by Marlborough's cavalry, who snapped up some hundreds of French prisoners (some reports say the entire Régiment de Montluc) and baggage wagons. However, Villeroi moved his army to shield Louvain and bad weather now intervened to hamper the Allied operations. It was only on 30 July that Marlborough was able to undertake a major crossing of the river, in the vicinity of Neerysche: 'We laid our tin boats over the Dyle.' Villeroi moved promptly to block the operation and the Dutch were reluctant to force a major action to sustain the advanced guard, which had already crossed to the far bank and were engaging the French with artillery. Frustrated, Marlborough pulled his troops back across the river, with little loss to either side, and moved his army into camp at Meldert, from where some useful time was spent in levelling the abandoned lines of defence. The Duke also took the chance to refresh his memory of the topography along the Ramillies watershed. As it happened, Villeroi had done the same, and one of the plans for possible action that he periodically submitted to Versailles for consideration actually included one for his army to fight a defensive battle on that very ridge.

A couple of weeks later Marlborough tried to engage Villeroi again. This time, by cutting loose from his supply bases and magazines and loading his carts with as much bread and ammunition as they could carry, he converted his army into an enormous flying column, able to move quickly and nimbly around the right flank of Villeroi's army as it lay covering Louvain. The Duke would be able to shrug off any counter-move by the French commander against his lines of supply and communication, at least for a few days. As it was, Villeroi was bemused by the sudden Allied dash to the south-west, across the headwaters of the Dyle, from where Marlborough could, if he chose, threaten Mons, Charleroi, Valenciennes or Brussels.

Marlborough had neatly forced the right flank of Villeroi, and his army, although living on tight rations, now stood between the Marshal and the French border. Villeroi moved a detachment under the Marquis de Grimaldi to the Yssche river, in order to cover the approaches to Brussels, but this force was badly outnumbered, as the main Allied army was soon seen advancing past Genappes through the Forest of Soignes. However, Grimaldi was in a fairly good defensive position, 'a deep muddy river in the front and the wood of Soignes in their rear ... close ground with hedges and ditches', but as yet the Marquis remained unsupported by Villeroi's main army, and was vulnerable to a well-pressed attack. There was some sharp skirmishing on 17 August, and on the following day Marlborough had a good chance to overwhelm the French detachment, before going on to confront a weakened Villeroi. To the Duke's intense annoyance, the Dutch were once again reluctant and insisted on holding a council of war to discuss the intended attack on Grimaldi. The following morning, when all had spoken, it was seen that Villeroi had closed his main army up to the Yssche position, which they had fortified in the night; no attack with a fair prospect of success was possible. There was little for Marlborough to do – commenting that he felt 'ten years older than I was a few days ago' – as the bread wagons were beginning to empty now, but withdraw back across the Dyle. He had to content himself with completing the spoiling of the Lines and laying siege to some minor French-held towns: 'The Duke detach'd General Schultz to the Siege of St Loewe ... and invested it around.'

In his disappointment, the Duke wrote to the Dutch States-General, complaining of the obstructive attitude of their generals, and also of the field deputies who accompanied the army: 'I flattered myself, that I might soon have congratulated Your High Mightinesses on a glorious victory ... the opportunity was too fair to let slip.' Marlborough hinted that he intended to retire, as his position was so much weaker than the previous year. The Dutch general officers and their deputy colleagues attempted to excuse their uncooperative behaviour by complaining to the States-General that Marlborough did not sufficiently consult them about his plans, that he 'without holding a council of war, made two or three marches for the execution of some design formed by His Grace, and we cannot conceal from your High Mightinesses that all the Generals of the army think it very strange.' In fact, as Marlborough knew very well, they were unable to keep things confidential even when they were told them. The Dutch had some grounds for complaint, however, given their own cautious inclination. The Duke hoped, by keeping his colleagues in the dark, to overcome their reluctance by springing a promising opportunity on them, one which would be too good to resist, to 'cheat them into a victory', as one of his correspondents perceptively put it. To their credit, however, the States-General saw that the situation could not carry on. Public opinion in Holland, robust and courageous, was outraged at the reports of the timidity of the Dutch generals and field deputies, and, a little reluctantly, the States recalled the most awkward of the deputies and transferred General Slangenberg, an undoubtedly very brave soldier but one whose conduct towards Marlborough had been particularly uncooperative, elsewhere.

To Villeroi, despite his own doubts, and an undoubted element of tactical fumbling in the last campaign, it seemed possible to believe that he had, in fact, foiled Marlborough. This encouraging tale grew in the telling as he wrote his dispatches to his friend the King in Versailles. The apparent success at blocking the Allied army at the crossings on the Dyle river, and 'forcing' the withdrawal from the forest of Soignes, was extolled, and scorn was heaped on the Duke and his efforts. The vital, crucially hampering part played by the cautious Dutch in ruining Marlborough's promising plans appears either not to have been recognized, or was conveniently ignored. Louis XIV, hungry for good tidings and eager to be convinced, readily accepted the Marshal's rather spurious claims and was pleased for him in his success. The French War Minister, Michel de Chamillart, visited Villeroi at this time and added his own dismissive comments on the Duke's abilities and performance, quickly coming to the dangerous conclusion that Marlborough's successes in Bavaria and at the Lines of Brabant (either of which occasions really should have been warning enough) were due more to good fortune than skill: 'I have a mediocre opinion of the capacity of the Duke of Marlborough.' A French diplomat also wrote at this time, 'We find in Holland that Monsieur de Marlborough is less successful at war than he was last year.'

After the awful events of 1704, France had recovered her strategic poise quite well during 1705. Marlborough's inability to achieve another major victory, despite undoubted successes at Huy and Elixheim, seemed significant. Marshal Villeroi's modestly successful campaign, added to Villars' skill in holding the Moselle valley secure, French advances in Spain and northern Italy, and the growing pressure that was exerted on Savoy (the recently joined and junior partner in the Grand Alliance) all seemed good indications that the Alliance was growing stale. The glittering opportunity gained at Blenheim seemed to have been allowed to pass. 'The last campaign', Colonel Jean-Martin De La Colonie wrote during the winter, 'had been so favourable to France, that she became convinced the wheel of fortune was turning in her favour.' Louis XIV was now putting out peace feelers, particularly to the Dutch, whose expenses in the war had so far been ruinous (and would become more so). It seemed for a while that the French King would succeed in driving a wedge between the main parties to the Grand Alliance, but the terms he suggested were so disproportionately unfavourable, given the events at Blenheim, that nothing came of the approach, for the time being. Importantly for Louis XIV, his own treasury was also in a sorry state; Blenheim had been an undoubted shock for him, and he would welcome a good peace that would enable his grandson to retain his domains in the Low Countries and on the throne in Madrid. Accordingly, in order to impress his enemies with the vitality of the French war effort and the huge resources that France could still call on, instructions flew out from Versailles to commanders in all theatres of war that, in the new campaigning season in the spring, France was to take the offensive everywhere. The King wrote to his generals: 'I can think of nothing which can better induce them [the Allies] to come to an agreement which has become necessary now than to let them see that I have sufficient forces to attack them everywhere.' All depended on the French commanders producing victory for their King; this was a dangerous course, and would inevitably diffuse the French war effort, with consequent dire results, not only in Flanders and in Italy but, to a lesser degree, in Spain as well.

Marlborough was not yet to know all this, having kept busy through the winter months with a series of diplomatic visits to the supporters of the Alliance, amongst them the Elector of the Palatinate, who was persuaded to send a large contingent of troops to bolster the Allied campaign in northern Italy. Operating in concert with the Dutch in the Low Countries, Marlborough despaired of ever achieving very much at all. On 26 March 1706, evidently feeling that little of consequence was to be expected in the coming year, he wrote:

> *The placing of the King of France's Household* [cavalry] *so that they may be sent either to Germany or Flanders is a plain instance that they intend to take their motions from what we shall do, which confirms me in my opinion of their being resolved to act in both places defensively.*

As a result, the Duke devised plans for a fresh attempt to advance into France through the Moselle valley (always, with good reason, in many ways his pet project), where

Marshal Marsin had recently taken up the command, and he also considered going to the upper Rhine frontier to join forces with the Margrave of Baden and so to threaten Alsace. That the Duke even thought, however briefly, of working with the awkward Margrave, who had given such trouble in the Danube campaign and then not turned up for the Moselle operations the following year, illustrates how frustrated he was and how doubtful he had become of finding success alongside the Dutch. He even considered a plan, which the States-General did not yet know about, to go and combine his British troops with those of with Prince Eugene in northern Italy, in an echo, almost, of the 1704 Danube campaign.

Marlborough took ship aboard the galley HMS *Peregrine*, landing in Holland on 14 April 1706, but the war in the wider sense soon took a turn for the worse, when news came in that the Duc de Vendôme had defeated an Imperial army at Calcinato in Italy on 19 April. French forces moved on to threaten Turin and the Duchy of Savoy. Then, in early May, Baden (who still suffered from a wound to the foot received in July 1704 at the Schellenberg battle) was defeated near Landau on the upper Rhine by Marshal Villars, who had been reinforced by Marsin with troops from the Moselle valley. Baden lost his lines of defence and important depots and magazines, and had to try and reform his battered army to the east of the river. With so many reverses, and with French military power apparently reinvigorated in response to Louis XIV's urging, the Dutch refused even to consider the Duke's leaving their borders, whether the Moselle valley (where Marsin was now a ready target after reinforcing Villars), the upper Rhine or Italy was the destination. In the interest of harmony amongst the Allies, Marlborough most reluctantly (although how serious the Italy project ever was is uncertain) shelved the schemes and looked forward again, with no enthusiasm, to a fresh campaign in the Low Countries.

Marlborough was also aware that the full concentration of his own army was delayed. Many Dutch officers had not yet rejoined their units, and arrears of pay for the Danish mounted troops were outstanding. Their King, not unreasonably, would not approve their use until these were settled. At the same time the King of Prussia was pursuing private quarrels with both the Imperial court in Vienna and the States-General at The Hague, and kept his troops in their quarters behind the Rhine while the disputes rumbled on. The Duke wrote in some exasperation to Lord Raby, Queen Anne's ambassador in Berlin, that 'If it should please God to give us a victory over the enemy, the Allies will be little obliged to the King; and if, on the other hand, we should have any disadvantage, I know not how he will be able to excuse himself.' Meanwhile, George, the Elector of Hanover, was being uncooperative and his troops were not ready to take the field, while negotiations for fresh contingents of Hessian troops were not progressing well. As if all this was not enough, there was a continuing worry about the adequate supply of horses for the Allied army; Marlborough's remount officers were scouring, amongst other regions, Schleswig-Holstein, Pomerania and the Protestant cantons of Switzerland for suitable supplies.

For all these gloomy considerations, there was one ray of hope for the Duke. It was rumoured in the Allied camp that Marshal Marsin was now sending cavalry reinforcements northwards to join the French army in the Low Countries, and that he had moved his headquarters to Metz, ready to march with his whole army and combine with Villeroi. If that were so (and the reports were soon afterwards confirmed), then Villeroi might feel confident enough to venture out and challenge Marlborough. In fact, as part of Louis XIV's desire to show a brave front to his opponents, the Marshal had recently received several letters from Versailles, urging him to do just that. Villeroi soon became quite concerned that the King suspected him of hanging back, at a time when Vendôme and Villars were operating in Italy and on the upper Rhine to such good effect. 'He had the feeling that the King doubted his courage, since he judged it necessary to spur him so hard', wrote the Duc de St Simon. Still, Marlborough had no great confidence that Villeroi really would advance to seek battle. He had always found the Marshal elusive and cautious, and he feared that he would, once again, cling to the protection of the river lines and avoid battle, as he had done in previous campaigns.

The Duke left The Hague on 9 May 1706 to join his steadily gathering army, and wrote, in some exasperation, to a friend in London six days later:

> When I left The Hague on Sunday, I was assured I would find the army in a condition to march, but as yet neither the artillery nor the bread-wagons are come so that we shall be obliged to stay [and wait] for the English, which will join us on Wednesday [19 May] and then we shall advance ... I go with a heavy heart, for I have no prospect of doing anything considerable unless the French would do what I am very confident they will not.

The British troops made good time and joined the army a day earlier than the Duke expected, on the Tuesday. This promptness, resulting from an improvement in the recent poor weather, was just as well, as events would prove. The Duke moved Overkirk's Dutch troops to Tongres, not far from Maastricht, although the Danish and Prussian units, whose fine performance had been such a feature of the previous campaigns, had still not joined the army. He added a note to his letter: 'The foreign troops I have seen are not so good as they were last year, but I hope the English are better.'

In the meantime, the French had apparently uncovered a plot by a prominent citizen of Namur, a Monsieur Pasgieur (or Pasgini in some accounts), to betray the city to the Allies. Whatever unpleasant fate befell the gentleman concerned, at the end of a noose, under the headsman's sword or on the wheel, is not known for certain, but nothing came of the plan itself, if it existed at all. However, Villeroi was sensitive to indications that Marlborough intended to open his new campaign along the line of the Meuse, and when the French commander marched, he would naturally incline to the south, both to be in a good position to counter any Allied attempt on Namur, and also to take practical advantage of the Taviers–Ramillies–Offuz watershed. Possession of this valuable geographical feature would enable the French commander either to move eastwards onto the plateau of Jandrenouille, and so interpose his army firmly between the Duke and the Meuse, or to stand and hold the ridge-line itself, denying its use to Marlborough. From that stout, seemingly unassailable, defensive position the French commander would also be able to threaten Marlborough's flank if he tried to press on towards Namur. This would effectively check the Duke's advance, and leave Villeroi with a number of promising options to pursue. It would all have seemed very pleasing and plausible.

In the circumstances, Villeroi was responding in a perfectly satisfactory way to the persistent urging from Versailles to take action. However, to the Marshal's natural wish to demonstrate his energy to the King and so take the field, and his own reasonable concern for the security of Namur if that really was Marlborough's intended victim, should be added the Duke's own avid desire for a decisive outright battle, wherever Villeroi could be found and got to stand and fight. The coming clash, if not at Ramillies then some other convenient point nearby, can be seen, almost, as an inevitability.

Chapter 2

WE MAY HAVE A COMPLETE VICTORY

O N 18 MAY 1706 Marshal Villeroi's army, which comprised 60,000 troops with sixty-two guns and an engineer bridging train of thirty-four pontoons (now that the cavalry reinforcements from the Moselle valley had arrived) began to move forward from the vicinity of Louvain, crossing the Dyle river to challenge the Duke of Marlborough. Confidence was high, the army was well trained and superbly equipped, and the generals were heartened, both by the belief that Marlborough's success in 1704 had been due to luck rather than skill, evidenced by his comparative lack of success the following year, and the certain knowledge that the contingents of Prussian, Hanoverian and Danish troops had not yet joined the Duke's army. Villeroi at first moved towards Tirlemont, as if the intention was to threaten Leau, abandoned by the French after the fight at Elixheim the previous summer; he then turned his army southwards, heading for Judoigne. This line of march took the French and Bavarian army towards the dry ground between the Mehaigne and Petite Gheete rivers. This was 'a narrow aperture of but 1200 paces' close to the small villages of Taviers and Ramillies (as Dutch engineers had described it three years earlier, when warning Marlborough of the folly of engaging the French in that vicinity), but which offered easy passage for marching troops between the small but marshy rivers in the area.

Marlborough learned from his cavalry scouts of the French advance the day after it began, and set about completing the concentration of the two separate Wings of his army. As Villeroi was apparently now moving to the south and east, it was almost inevitable that both commanders would soon be looking to gain the dry ground between the Petite Gheete and the Mehaigne before their opponent got there. Clearly the Allied and French armies would be marching on a collision course, something that the Duke, in particular, welcomed after the frustration and disappointment of the previous year. Now, much more cooperative after the Duke's very real anger with them in the autumn of 1705 and his written protests to the States-General, the Dutch deputies and their generals would place no hindrance in his way. Through the simple demands of geography and the physical need for firm passage for large bodies of marching soldiers, there was a certain inevitability about the choice of ground for the coming clash of arms. Both commanders, for quite different reasons, were seeking battle, and their armies each needed the dry ground to advance in good order. In the circumstances, a collision at Ramillies was no real surprise; John Millner wrote of the two commanders, 'they striving and the Allies also, who should first possess themselves of Ramalies and the strong ground thereabout.' Despite this, neither Marlborough nor Villeroi quite appreciated how far his opponent had got on the march, each expecting to gain the Ramillies watershed first; the two armies, it might fairly be said, would soon stumble into one another.

Meanwhile, Marlborough had combined the troops in British pay at Bitsen with Veldt Marshal Overkirk's forces, which had gathered at Tongres just to the south of Maastricht. The Duke also wrote with an appeal to the Duke of Württemberg, the commander of the Danish contingent: 'I send you this express to request your Highness to bring forward by a double march your cavalry so as to join us at the earliest moment, letting your infantry follow with all speed possible without exhaustion.' The Duke included in his urgent message an assurance that the still outstanding arrears of pay would be made good, and astutely phrased the wording so that, if Württemberg should not be at hand

Marshal Villeroi

*Born in April 1644, François de
Neufville, Duc de Villeroi was the son
of a noble French family that first
came to prominence in the reign of
King Charles IX. His father, Nicholas
de Neufville, had been the governor of
Louis XIV when he was a minor,
and François and the Sun King
remained close friends,
having known each other
since those early, troubled
times. Villeroi was a
polished courtier, an
elegant, witty and
cultured man. His military
career was long and quite
distinguished, if not
spectacular, and in 1695 during
the Williamite wars he succeeded
Marshal Luxembourg on that soldier's
death as commander of the French
armies in the Low Countries. Villeroi,
who had a reputation for great
personal bravery, was made a Marshal
of France at this time, although he
found William III to be a formidable
opponent, and his efforts against the
Dutchman were rather unsuccessful.*

*Prior to the outbreak of the War of
the Spanish Succession, Villeroi was
sent by Louis XIV to northern Italy as
army commander, in place of Marshal
Catinat, but his army was beaten in
1701 by the Imperial troops, led by
Prince Eugene, at Chiari. Soon
afterwards he allowed his army to be
surprised in its camp at Cremona and
the Marshal was taken prisoner,
although he was exchanged before
very long. Villeroi campaigned in the
Spanish Netherlands against
Marlborough in 1703, and the
following year he shadowed the Duke's
march up the Rhine, joining Tallard in
Alsace before that Marshal went to*

*historic defeat at Blenheim in the
Danube valley. Villeroi moved forward
into the Black Forest to help extricate
Marshal Marsin's battered army and
the fugitive remnants of the Elector of
Bavaria's forces in the wake of that
disaster, and this was a well-handled
if unglamorous operation, which is
generally overlooked.*

*During 1705 Villeroi once
again commanded the
French army in the Low
Countries, and
conducted a successful
campaign, despite one
or two close calls,
foiling Marlborough's
efforts either to seize
large amounts of territory
or pin his opponent down to
battle in open field. Urged on by
Louis XIV to confront Marlborough in
May 1706, however, Villeroi was
soundly defeated at Ramillies by the
Duke, who was an incomparably finer
commander. On his return to
Versailles, Villeroi was kindly received
by the French King, but was never
again offered a military command,
instead assuming the role of courtier
and confidant of the monarch once
more.*

*In 1714 Villeroi was made a
Minister of State, and during the
minority of Louis XV he was governor
and mentor to the young King. He fell
from favour after scheming against
the volatile Regent, the King's uncle,
the Duc d'Orléans, who had Villeroi
arrested by officers of the
Mousquetaires Gris, and
unceremoniously bundled away from
court in a sedan chair. The Marshal
was subsequently made governor of
Lyons, almost a post of internal exile
for such an eminent person, where he
died in July 1730.*

to read the note immediately, any competent staff officer would not hesitate but get the Danish troops marching, while the commander was found and asked to give the actual orders for such a movement: 'In case Your Highness is not with the leading corps, the officer commanding that corps is hereby instructed to march without waiting further orders, and to forward this letter to Your Highness and all commanders in rear so that they also can conform.' In the event, Württemberg responded magnificently to the message, and his twenty-one squadrons of Danish cavalry joined the army just in time for the coming battle. John Deane of the 1st English Foot Guards wrote that 'the Danish troops came up with our reere this evening [22 May] and campt at a small distance from us.' Marlborough's order of battle was still not complete, though, and with several scores of Dutch officers on leave at home the battle would have to be fought without them. Despite this lack, the 62,000-strong Allied army – 74 infantry battalions and 123 squadrons of cavalry – when the Danes joined, accompanied by 90 pieces of artillery and 20 mortars and howitzers, together with a bridging train of 42 pontoons, was moving rapidly southwards on 21 May, although Marlborough slowed his progress by a full day near Corswaren, to allow the Danish squadrons to catch up: 'I hope they may be with us on Saturday', he wrote to a friend in London. In delaying in this way until 22 May, he briefly surrendered the initiative to Villeroi, who got to the crucial ground first as a result. This was a very brief and shallow advantage for the Marshal, but it was an advantage all the same. What mattered far more were the reactions of the two opposing commanders when the actual clash came. With the armies more or less in balance numerically and equal in the capabilities of their weapons and tactics, which of the two men would make good decisions the faster? Whose touch in command of his army would be the more sure,

Veldt Marshal Henry of Nassau, Count Overkirk, who commanded the Dutch cavalry at Ramillies.

whose procedures were best? The general who took control, who got a telling punch in first and then held the initiative and dictated the action, would win.

That Marlborough foresaw, and welcomed, the coming battle is shown in a letter he wrote to the States-General on 21 May, less than forty-eight hours before the fateful clash:

The French, having drained all their garrisons, had passed the Dyle and were come to the camp at Tirlemont, which you may believe has quite broken the measures we were projecting at Maastricht; so that upon this news the army marched yesterday from Tongres hither; where the English joined us, and to-morrow we expect the Danes; then we design to advance to gain the head of the Gheete [the Taviers–Ramillies watershed] *to come to the enemy if they keep their ground* [the Duke's concern that Villeroi would, as in 1705, shy away at the last moment is plain]. *For my part, I can think of nothing more happy for the Allies than a battle, since I have good reason to hope, with the blessing of God, we may have a complete victory.*

However, the Duke plainly expected to get across the Ramillies watershed and meet Villeroi in the vicinity of Judoigne; he was not yet aware that the French commander had advanced with his army quite as far forward as he had done.

The weather had been bad in recent weeks, with the rains making the roads muddy, but these were drying steadily and the armies made good time (also allowing, incidentally, the Danish troops to come up with no delays, enabling Marlborough to concentrate most of his force). So, in the early morning of Whit Sunday 23 May 1706, the French army approached from the west the low ridge-line running from Ramillies northwards to the villages of Offuz and Autre-Eglise. Just beyond Ramillies, to the south of the village, was a mile and a half wide open plain stretching to Taviers, offering the coveted dry passage when moving

Maximilien-Emmanuel Wittelsbach, Elector of Bavaria. He hurried from Pentecostal celebrations to command Villeroi's left Wing at Ramillies.

from east to west. Marshal Villeroi was first on the ground, and plainly expected that a clash with Marlborough would take place, for the Irish soldier of fortune Peter Drake, serving with the French army in the Régiment de Courrière, remembered that sixteen rounds of ball ammunition had been issued that very morning against just such an eventuality (an interesting clue to the degree of firepower expected to be generated in a general action at the time). Despite this, Villeroi's cavalry commander, Maximilien-Emmanuel Wittelsbach, the renegade Elector of Bavaria and Governor General of the Spanish Netherlands, was absent in Brussels that Sunday, attending Pentecostal celebrations. He would not catch up with the army until later in the day; he would, however, arrive in time to fight for his life before nightfall.

Across the marshy valley of the Petite Gheete stream from the marching French and Bavarian army, lay the plateau of Jandrenouille, and cantering across the turf came William Cadogan, Marlborough's burly Irish Quartermaster General, riding westwards through the early morning drizzle and mist with a cavalry escort of 700 dragoons, 'the correct number for the purpose', looking for a camping ground for the night near Ramillies. The Allied army was still at their snatched breakfast several miles to the east, having spent much of the night in damp bivouacs in the area between Corswaren and Merdorp, and their intention was to move forward, past Ramillies and Taviers, to occupy the plateau of Mont St André, to the west of the watershed. From here, Marlborough would be well placed to close with the French army, thought to be still near Judoigne a little to the north and, with good fortune, bring them to battle before they could retire behind the Dyle once again.

Plainly, Marlborough was not aware that Villeroi had come quite so far forward, and the Marshal, in this respect at least, seems to have been one step ahead, quite literally, of the Duke. At about 7 a.m. Cadogan's dragoon escort clashed with some French cavalry troopers, who were gathering forage on the edge of the plateau of Jandrenouille. After a brief exchange of shots, the foragers drew off to the west, so Cadogan pressed forward, and was soon able to make out the smartly ordered lines of Villeroi's army as it moved majestically beyond the Ramillies–Offuz ridge-line, preparing to deploy across the watershed; as Colonel Jean-Martin De La Colonie wrote, 'We were able to march our army on a broad front as we desired, and the result was a magnificent spectacle ... France had surpassed herself in

William, 1st Earl Cadogan. Allied Quartermaster General, the first to see the French army in position at Ramillies.

the quality of these troops.' He remarked to a companion, that 'if defeated now, we could never again hope to withstand them.'

Alerted by reports of the brief cavalry clash on the edge of the plateau of Jandrenouille, the French commander quickly moved to deploy his army along the four miles of frontage from Taviers in the south, across the broad crop-covered plain to Ramillies village and on to the enclosed gardens and orchards around Offuz and Autre-Eglise in the north, where 'runs the river Geet, which makes the ground in most places very swampy.' That the Allied army was on the move would have come as no surprise to the French, although the Marshal, like Marlborough, appears not to have appreciated quite how close the two armies had come together before this initial contact was made. Villeroi could have derived some satisfaction from the sure knowledge that he was first on the ground. 'Coming in sight of the enemy', Peter Drake wrote, 'the cannon was ordered to the front to be placed on proper ground to annoy them.' Getting the cumbersome pieces with their oxen teams into place, even on firm ground, was a time-consuming procedure, and apart from some ranging shots by both sides, more or less at random, there was no real artillery work done until that afternoon.

Cadogan meanwhile sent messengers hurrying back to Merdorp to bring Marlborough forward to a position from where he could view the French army for himself. The Duke, accompanied by the Dutch field commander Veldt Marshal Overkirk, General Daniel Dopff and some staff officers, joined Cadogan at about 10 a.m., by which time the mist had conveniently risen, allowing them a full and uninterrupted view of Villeroi's unfolding dispositions. Along with the party was a newly joined Dutch field deputy, Sicco van Goslinga, a very brave but rather opinionated man, who would prove to be a sore trial to Marlborough over the next few years. He apparently pointed out that:

The enemy's left could not be attacked with any prospect of success; for the hedges, ditches and marshes were a complete barrier to both sides; that therefore the whole of our cavalry should be massed on our left, even if they had to be three or four lines deep there.

The Duke accepted the civilian deputy's lecture with a polite smile, and promptly ignored his advice. To show his hand so soon, and so plainly, to his opponent would be folly, even if the exact details of his own plan was not, as it could not reasonably be, fully formed at this early stage in the proceedings; a lot would depend on Villeroi's reaction to the first shock of Marlborough's attack. The open plain to the south of Ramillies was, in any case, the obvious place to mass the bulk of the Allied cavalry, and the Marshal would do the same, for precisely the same tactical reason; the more broken ground to the north of Ramillies offered

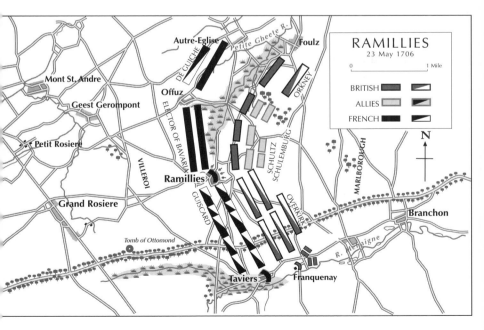

Ramillies, deployment phase.

limited scope for effective cavalry action, although it would prove to be not entirely impassable to horsemen.

Aware of the Marshal's knack over the previous eighteen months of drawing off and avoiding battle, and concerned not to let the chance slip away this time, Marlborough hastily called forward his leading echelons of cavalry to close up to the French as near as could be without actually bringing on a premature general engagement, while the Allied army was not yet ready to support them. This cavalry advance, confident and forthright but not rash, would fix Villeroi in position and force him to commit to a fight that day. If he tried to draw off, the French commander risked an escalating and damaging running battle with Marlborough's cavalry, something that could very easily tumble out of control amidst all the confusion of his baggage train, before he could get his army back to the shelter of the Dyle river. If, on the other hand, the French and Bavarian troops on the other side of the stream were just an advanced guard, without real support, that had pushed on too far and too fast, then the Allied squadrons could give them a good mauling without too much trouble. Villeroi might then be obliged to come forward to save his detachment from destruction, and, in turn, become obliged to stand and fight. As it was, it was very soon apparent to the Duke that the main French force, in all its might, was a short distance away over there, massing its strength to meet the advancing Allied army.

Marlborough was also accompanied on his reconnaissance to the edge of the plateau of Jandrenouille by a number of Walloon officers familiar with the region. They also warned him that the ground to the north, where the stream of the Petite Gheete stretched from Ramillies and Offuz to Autre-Eglise and beyond, was too marshy to be crossed in the face of any determined opposition, and therefore it was not practical to try and attack in that area. The Duke, who was well aware of this problem, having scouted the area with care the previous year after the fight at Elixheim, paid no more attention to them than he had to deputy Goslinga's hints. As his army came forward, deploying from ponderous columns of march into eight nimble columns of attack, moving forward in the well-practised manoeuvre to form a line of battle, the soldiers found themselves marching over the debris of the demolished Lines of Brabant, a work at which they had laboured the previous autumn. Just a few miles to the north was the old battlefield of Landen, and the older, veteran, soldiers in the Allied army may well have remembered the awful carnage of that day in 1693 as they tramped forward to action once again. The Duke directed the British cavalry and infantry towards Autre-Eglise in the northern sector, while the Dutch and Danish squadrons went to the south, to face the French cavalry, which could be seen massing on the open plain between Ramillies and Taviers. Nineteen battalions of Dutch infantry supported Overkirk's horsemen, while, in the centre, brigades of Dutch along with German, Protestant Swiss and Scots troops in the

The plateau of Jandrenouille. Marlborough's army advanced to battle across these fields.

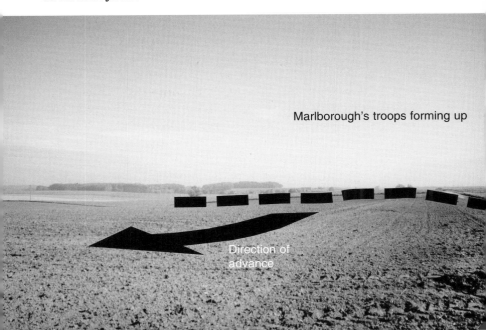

Marlborough's troops forming up

Direction of advance

Dutch service closed up to Ramillies itself; here Marlborough had a great battery of thirty 24-pounder guns (some reports say twenty guns) dragged into position by teams of oxen, ready to open fire on the French guns (some of which were of a rather peculiar three-barrel design first seen the previous year at Elixheim), which were already being deployed around the village.

On the other side of the tactical hill, Villeroi arranged his army with competent skill; the topography lent itself quite well to defensive action, with the natural bias of cavalry on the right and infantry on the left. The bulk of the powerful French cavalry, eighty-two squadrons in all, commanded that day by the able veteran, General de Guiscard, were deployed on the plain in the south. The elite Maison du Roi cavalry and the red-coated Gendarmerie formed up as the front ranks, where their skill and mobility could be put to best effect on the wide cornfields, while brigades of French, Swiss and Bavarian infantry were ranged in their support. Additional batteries were placed on the edge of Ramillies, ready to sweep the open field towards Taviers, where, presumably, the intention must have been also to site guns. (Some reports mention artillery actually being in Taviers, but most, in particular the narrative left by Colonel De La Colonie, do not.) The boggy ground of the Mehaigne stream, on the far right, should also provide protection against any Allied flanking movement. Meanwhile, Ramillies village on the other side of the plain, at this time a meagre cluster of thatched cottages, one or two substantial houses and walled farms, and a church, would provide an anchor for the left flank of de Guiscard's squadrons. Overall, in the south of the field, this was as it ought to be, with a balanced mix of cavalry (benefiting from good, firm going) and infantry, backed by powerful and well-sited artillery; all should be well, with careful management, and de Guiscard was certainly regarded as a 'safe pair of hands' with the experience and skill to direct the battle here. The

Marshal, however, had inexplicably neglected to properly clear away the baggage wagons and camp equipment and the attendant followers of the army, and these were allowed to clutter the area immediately along the French and Bavarian line of battle, 'heaped up between the two lines', as the Marquis de Feuquières remembered. At the time this would have seemed of little importance, a minor administrative untidiness which could be attended to later, although it would plainly have been good practice to clear the whole area of wagons.

A little to the north of Ramillies, where the marshes of the Petite Gheete stream made the going difficult, Walloon and Bavarian infantry occupied the orchards and fields of the low ridge-line running from Ramillies to Offuz and on to Autre-Eglise at the left of the position, where woods and broken country covered that flank. In their support, on the plateau of Mont St André, stood the Elector's fifty massed squadrons of Bavarian and Walloon cavalry (although four squadrons of Bavarian cuirassiers were sent south to support de Guiscard on the plain, taking up a position on the left of the squadrons of the Maison du Roi). The villages of Autre-Eglise in the north, and Ramillies and Offuz in the centre, were all packed with infantry and put into a state of defence, with the alleys barricaded and the cottages and walled farms loop-holed for muskets, as was Taviers in the south. Villeroi disposed his artillery with care, although the field of fire in the north, where the Petite Gheete valley dipped away immediately to the front, was rather limited. The powerful batteries he established near Ramillies in the centre, however, suffered no such disadvantage, and they enjoyed good arcs of fire, able to fully cover the approaches from the edge of the plateau of Jandrenouille, which the Allied infantry would have to cross to come to grips. Captain Robert Parker of the Royal Irish Regiment rather dismissively wrote that 'along this river to the villages of Offuse and Autreglise which covered their left flank, was posted a thin line of the worst of their infantry, with squadrons after a scattering manner in their rear.' The captain was rather mistaken in his scornful assessment or in his memory of Villeroi's dispositions, and having been involved in the infantry action there he perhaps should have known this. The stout defence mounted by the French and Walloon infantry, as will be seen, would put the British troops to a severe test before the afternoon was over.

As it turned out, the lie of the land, in a silent and subtly destructive way, actually worked against Marshal Villeroi, no matter how much care he took to arrange his army; yet the French commander had little notion that this was so. Tactically, it was imperative that he throw his flanks forward to occupy the villages of Taviers on the right and Autre-

The Ramillies–Offuz ridge-line, seen from Marlborough's forming-up point.

Eglise on the left; this all made sense, and he could do no less, unless his army was to be exposed to a turning movement. By adopting this extended defensive posture his commanders were, in fact, obliged to fatally overstretch themselves. In the face of such an accomplished opponent as Marlborough, this was risky. 'The position he had taken up', wrote the Duc de St Simon, 'was well known to be bad.' For his opponent, the broken ground to the north offered an obstacle to easy movement and narrowed the usable frontage, obliging Marlborough to, apparently, take the most obvious course, and deploy his cavalry on the left, where it was awaited by the powerful bulk of the French squadrons of the Maison du Roi, already settled comfortably into position. So, the curious fact was that both generals were deploying for battle on ground which, it was popularly believed, was not suited to the type of operation

they each chose to undertake – defence for the Frenchman, attack for the Englishman.

All this while Marlborough's army was closing up to the French: 'our army arrived in full view of the enemy, and about Noon came in cannon-shot thereof.' The Duke, with his slight numerical advantage, took care to ensure that the Allied battle line occupied a smaller frontage than that of their opponents. This tight, potent formation (which was almost certainly no accident) had a double advantage, for the Allied blow, when it came, would be more concentrated and carry more weight. Also, due to the awkward topography of the battlefield, Villeroi had, in quite rightly occupying Taviers in the south and Autre-Eglise in the north, unavoidably thrown his flanks forward, and as a result his army stood in battle array in a shallow arc formation. Had he chosen to do so, the Marshal could have tried to envelop the flanks of the Allies as they deployed for battle off the plateau of Jandrenouille. Such an ambitious course, which would threaten Marlborough with an encirclement battle, called for an early decision, and was at odds with Villeroi's rather sedate character. He chose instead to dig in his heels and wait for Marlborough's attack, not in itself a bad tactical decision. This meant, though, that the French and Bavarians would have to stand the shock of the first Allied attack, in this way letting their opponents exhaust themselves on the solid defences, with Villeroi then moving forward in counterattack, perhaps picking up the encirclement battle option once more. Given the natural strength of the position, and that the Duke had only a very slight advantage in numbers, the French commander's decisions were perfectly satisfactory and justifiable. As with the situation to the south of Ramillies, where the French cavalry required adequate infantry support both to hold their ground and to protect their flank in the marshes along the Mehaigne, careful and active management was required to maintain the advantages offered by the position and Villeroi's success in getting in place before Marlborough had done.

An unnoticed advantage offered by Marlborough's narrower frontage (given that Villeroi made no move to envelop his flanks) was that Allied soldiers could be moved from one side of the field to the other by 'cutting across the middle of the chord', whereas Villeroi's troops would have to take the long route, marching around the outside of the arc, if they tried to do the same thing. This tactical handicap, initially so slight as to merit almost no attention, would grow in importance as the events of the afternoon unfolded, and was commented on by the Duc de St Simon: 'There was a marsh which covered our left, but prevented our two wings from joining.' The possible threat of Villeroi throwing forward his army in a converging attack at the flanks of the Allied army as it deployed, remained just that, a possibility, and caused the Duke no real concern. He judged his man well, for Villeroi was digging in his heels to fight a defensive battle on the ridge-line. If he was not going to move forward and attack Marlborough on the plateau of Jandrenouille, the Marshal must fight and win there on the watershed. An orderly withdrawal under pressure was not open to him, with all the baggage of his army just to the rear of the French line of battle. Marlborough, much more agile in his approach, retained the option to advance to the attack, to stand and invite a French attack on himself, or retire to the eastward and seek battle on another occasion (although to have done so would be against all his instincts and desire to engage in a decisive battle).

While the two armies made their dispositions and dragged their big guns into place, the morning sped by, and a bright sunny afternoon came on. The hours before noon had by no means been devoid of action, as skirmishes and clashes broke out along the length of the line, where the troops jostling to get into position had, occasionally, to push off the unwelcome inquisitive attention of their opponents. Lord Ailesbury, an exiled Jacobite who lived nearby (and was an old friend of Marlborough), remembered the morning well, and wrote, 'Rising sooner than usual, we went to a hollow way just near the convent where we heard the musket shot most plain.'

Villeroi had at last been joined by the Elector of Bavaria, fresh from church attendance in Brussels, who went to command the cavalry in the north. Across the valley,

Marlborough had completed his own close reconnaissance and deployed his army, and so, shortly before 2 p.m., he gave the order. The massed Allied batteries opened fire, and Villeroi's gunners responded immediately, pounding the Dutch and German infantry brigades squaring up to Ramillies village, as a terrific artillery duel broke out along the four-mile length of the line. Richard Kane wrote, 'Our cannon being placed as most proper, they began cannonading and playing against the enemy, and there's against us, very vigorous and smart on both sides.' Drifting smoke quickly began to obscure the battlefield, particularly to the north, where lay the broken country along the Petite Gheete; the fog of war, physical and psychological, inevitable and all but impenetrable to other than the keenest minds, settled over the field. The general who proved to be the more alert would be at a distinct advantage.

Chapter 3

ALMOST AS MURDEROUS AS THE REST

ON THE FAR RIGHT of the French line of battle that Sunday afternoon, the small village of Taviers, sitting amidst the marshes of the Mehaigne river and its tributary, the Visoule stream, had been occupied by two battalions of the Greder Suisse Régiment in the French service. This place had a particular importance for the French commander – although Marshal Villeroi seems to have paid very little attention to it at all – both to protect the otherwise unsupported flank of General de Guiscard's cavalry on the open plain, and at the same time to exert a threat to the flank of the Dutch and Danish cavalry squadrons as they came forward into position under command of Veldt Marshal Overkirk. This could be particularly effective if the French had taken the trouble to establish artillery batteries in the area around the village, to catch the Allied cavalry in enfilade fire as they attempted to form up. Artillery positioned around Taviers would not achieve overlapping fire (the ideal) with their counterparts on the edge of Ramillies, where their batteries were already in place, but they could still have done a lot of useful damage to Overkirk's horsemen. These guns could have left little of the plain unswept by French artillery, and impeded the advance of the Allied left, going some way to redress the imbalance brought about by the relative, and growing, lack of proper infantry support for de Guiscard's cavalry as the battle developed.

Despite this weakness in his arrangements, the French commander's attention was now almost entirely devoted elsewhere, to the north of the battlefield, where the British cavalry, dragoons and infantry, conspicuous in their red coats, were now very visibly deploying. In this more broken country, the French and Bavarian artillery was of less use, and the gunners, for all their skill, were soon reduced to an expensive and entirely unproductive artillery duel with Marlborough's batteries around Ramillies and along the edge of the plateau of Jandrenouille. Louis XIV had written to Villeroi on 6 May 1706: 'Have particular care to that part of the line which will endure the first shock of the English troops', and the Elector of Bavaria had once warned, 'Beware of these men, they are dangerous.' Heeding this advice, at this early stage the Marshal was beginning to move infantry battalions away from the support of de Guiscard's cavalry, to bolster the position held by the Elector's troops on the ridge-line between Ramillies, Offuz and Autre-Eglise. This was already a naturally strong position, shielded to the front by the bogs of the Petite Gheete stream and by rising ground which, while not particularly steep to the ridge-line, was broken up with orchards and gardens, a good place to fight a defensive infantry battle. The bold advance of the British troops had its mesmerizing effect upon Villeroi, however, and on Marlborough's part this was probably quite intentional. Richard Kane remembered that:

> The Elector and Villeroy saw our right Wing
> marching down on their left, they were startled;
> whereupon they in a great hurry sent off from the plain
> a great many of their troops to sustain their left, which
> put the rest on the plain in some disorder.

A breakthrough there, on the French and Bavarian left, around Offuz and Autre-Eglise, would not only be serious in itself as a straightforward tactical problem on the field of battle but, if developed successfully, would threaten Villeroi's line of communication with the Dyle river and Louvain. The Marshal was certainly not going into action while looking over his left shoulder to a potential line of retreat; he intended and expected to win that day. All the same, a move by his opponents to turn his left flank appeared to be a more urgent threat than any corresponding threat to his right, where the power and mobility of de Guiscard's fine cavalry could be deployed to good effect on the wonderful open country, ideal for mounted action, to the south. So, significantly less attention was paid by the French commander to the rapidly unfolding situation on the plain.

It was now apparent that the French had not taken the chance that morning to occupy and fortify the small hamlet of Franquenay, on the same muddy stream and just a few hundred yards forward of Taviers. It was a position now vulnerable to seizure by the approaching waves of Dutch infantry in their blue uniforms with orange facings, who had been gathering for some time on the edge of Boneffe a mile or so to the east. Rather belatedly, soon after midday, several companies of Swiss troops had been hurried forward from Taviers to occupy the cottages and barns of Franquenay. Soldiers were placed to line the adjacent hedges and gardens, but they were without real support – no guns or cavalry squadrons stood nearby, and they were too far ahead of Taviers to be supported by their comrades there either. Hardly had the Swiss got into place when, at about 2 p.m., a brigade of Dutch Guards under command of Colonel Wertmüller (often, but incorrectly, referred to as General), came smartly forward from their forming up area, in a resolute attempt to seize Franquenay for themselves. The four Dutch battalions were supported by two light field guns (often attached to the infantry as 'battalion guns'), boldly manhandled forward by their crews, and these were firing canister-shot at close range into the exposed ranks of the heavily outnumbered defenders. Shaken by the brutal suddenness of the Dutch attack, the normally reliable Swiss, unsupported by the battalions to the rear, did not hold their ground. They were quickly driven out of Franquenay and fled back across the boggy pastures,

Taviers village and church, seized by Dutch infantry early on in the battle.

Two-pounder battalion gun. Used to devastating effect by the Dutch infantry at Taviers.

hampering the field of view and of fire of the troops in Taviers. Hardly had the fugitive Swiss rejoined their comrades, when the renewed assault of Wertmüller's Guards came in, and a vicious battle at bayonet point erupted through the alleys and in and about the cottages and barns of Taviers.

Aware that reinforcements were being hurried to their aid, the Swiss fought back with determination, refusing to be driven, and losses on both sides mounted quickly, which infuriated the soldiers in the close-quarter stabbing and clubbing contest. Colonel De La Colonie, standing with his regiment of grenadiers on the plain nearby, remembered that 'this village was the scene of the opening of the engagement, and the fighting there was almost as murderous as the rest of the battle put together.' Such a fierce contest could not last and the superiority in Dutch numbers and fire-power soon told; by about 3 p.m., Wertmüller's Guards had pushed the surviving Swiss soldiers right out of Taviers, into the marshes of the Visoule stream, where, in their confusion, they were exposed to the musketry of the triumphant Dutch. Suddenly, all was chaos on the right flank of Villeroi's army, now open and vulnerable, far away and out of sight of the French commander, who was absorbed with developments on his left; rapid action was required to restore the situation.

The French cavalry commander in the southern part of the battlefield, General de Guiscard, was soon alert to the unfolding peril, and he took prompt, if rather ill-judged, action to recover Taviers. He ordered a swift counterattack on the Dutch Guards by some of his own third-line troops, the fourteen squadrons of French dragoons, from the Le Roi, La Reine, Notat and d'Aubigni regiments, who at that time were standing with their horses in reserve near the peculiar hillock (or tumulus) known as the Tomb of Ottomonde. Two more battalions of the Greder Suisse Régiment, under command of Brigadier General de Nonan,

Colonel Jean-Martin De La Colonie

This accomplished French officer left highly informative memoirs of his service, both with the French army and on secondment to the Bavarian service during the War of the Spanish Succession. He had fought as a cadet in the French-Dutch wars of the 1690s and then served with a dragoon regiment before taking command of the Grenadiers Rouges. This was a rather motley unit in the Bavarian army, which was made up of deserters and other miscreants drawn from France, Savoy and Switzerland who volunteered to serve on rather than face imprisonment or the noose. Many of the officers in the regiment (although De La Colonie was not one of them) had similarly chequered histories, and had been given the opportunity to redeem their reputations in the line of battle rather than being dismissed in disgrace.

Despite the unpromising material from which the regiment was originally recruited (and the officers often had their hands full maintaining discipline), the Grenadiers Rouges proved to be a resilient lot, and they earned a thoroughly good reputation amongst both the Bavarians and the French for being tough fighters. Almost alone the regiment maintained its discipline at the Schellenberg battle in July 1704, when the rest of the defences fell to pieces in the face of the Duke of Marlborough's forthright assault. De La Colonie led the grenadiers at Ramillies and was involved in the failed counterattack in the southern part of the battlefield that laid the French and Bavarian flank open to the Danish cavalry. His intimate account of the fighting that day is amongst the best that can be found. De La Colonie subsequently took part in the actions at Oudenarde (1708), where his troops were not very much involved (although they held their position longer than most), and at Malplaquet (1709), where they were heavily engaged. After the end of the war De La Colonie took service with the Bavarians once again, this time to fight the Turks, before retiring to the family estates in France. His memoirs were translated into English and published in London in 1904.

were sent by the infantry commander on the plain, General de la Motte, in their support. However, due to laboriously having to thread their way through the massed ranks of the Maison du Roi cavalry in their well-ordered formations, the Swiss infantry lagged behind the dragoons as they moved towards Taviers. The counterattack, instead of having real punch, was given no proper attention, and as a consequence quickly became a piecemeal, poorly coordinated affair, and it failed miserably. 'The units were at some distance from each other in the first instance', De La Colonie recalled, 'and being uninformed as to whom they were to work with, each took their own line to reach the village, ignorant even as to whether there was a likelihood of its being defended.' Defended it undoubtedly was, as Opdham's and Holstein's regiments of dismounted Dutch dragoons had both moved forward to support Wertmüller's Guards, and together they poured in a heavy and merciless musketry fire upon the French dragoons as they struggled forward on foot in their long boots. The section of Dutch battalion guns added their canister fire at the same time, tumbling the dragoons down in large numbers. Colonel d'Aubigni, who led his regiment into the attack, was mortally wounded, their ranks wavered, and the leading squadrons of Württemberg's Danish cavalry, unhampered now by any fire either from Franquenay or Taviers, moved forward and cut swiftly in towards their exposed flank. John Millner wrote, 'Wirtemberg at the same time being arrived with some Danish squadrons slipt in between the Enemies left and Taviers, and flankt them, but by a marsh [the Visoule stream] in the way, he was obliged to stop a little.'

De La Colonie had received orders to move his Grenadiers Rouges, together with the Cologne Guards with whom they were brigaded, from their post to the south of Ramillies and support the faltering counterattack on Taviers. As with the Swiss, these troops had to make their way through the lines of cavalry, although the Colonel noticed that their ranks were somewhat thinner than was usual (de Guiscard had some difficulty covering his wide frontage to best effect and with real depth). The veterans amongst the troopers cheered the grenadiers as they marched southwards, however, 'waving their caps with grateful applause' and recalling their sterling performance at the Schellenberg fight in 1704, when alone of the French and Bavarian troops that day they had tried to stand firm as the defence of that hill collapsed in bloody disarray. However, as De La Colonie approached the marshy ground along the Mehaigne and Visoule streams, he could see that all was chaos ahead, as the advance of the dismounted French dragoons and their Swiss infantry supports had broken down in the face of the heavy Dutch fire and the movement of the Danish squadrons against their flank. Now his own brigade commander rode impetuously on ahead to test the depth of the marsh, but went in too far and almost immediately got his horse stuck in the mud, so that he was taken away as a prisoner by the Dutch. As a result, De La Colonie now found himself in command of the brigade, and he remembered that:

We crossed fairly easily on foot, though in some parts were over knee-deep in water. Scarcely had my troops got over when the dragoons and Swiss who had preceded us, came tumbling down upon my battalions in full flight, just at the time when I was re-forming my men after their crossing ... My own fellows turned about and fled along with them.

Indignant at this craven behaviour in his men, the Colonel called on them to rally, seizing the regimental colour from a dazed subaltern: 'I was never more surprised in my life to find myself standing alone with a few officers and the colours ... I cried out in German and in French like one possessed.'

Gathering together a small party of his nervous soldiers, De La Colonie drew them up at the edge of the Visoule

John Churchill, 1st Duke of Marlborough.

Courtesy of the late Dr David Chandler.

The Duke of Marlborough and the Quartermaster General, William Cadogan.

By kind permission of His Grace the Duke of Marlborough.

The cavalry action at Ramillies. Sketch by Louis Laguerre. Courtesy of The Marquess of Anglesey.

The Duke of Marlborough and his staff, overseeing the battle for Ramillies village. Courtesy of The Marquess of Anglesey.

Ramillies village from the plain to the south. The scene of the huge cavalry battle between de Guiscard's French, and the Dutch and the Danes under Overkirk.
Author's collection.

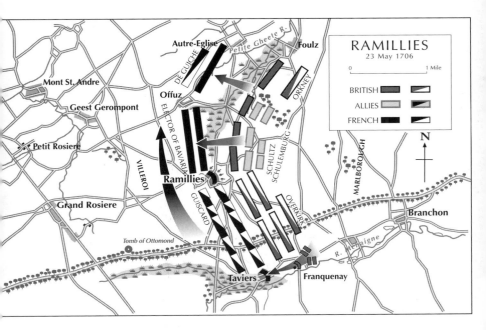

Ramillies, attack phase 1.

stream just to the west of Taviers, from where they managed to extricate some of the dismounted French dragoons from the marshy ground, who were now providing target practice for the Dutch Guards. With a scratch force of his own grenadiers, who sheepishly came back into line around the Colonel and the colour party, and the remnants of the French dragoons and the Greder Suisse battalions, De La Colonie was able to provide some, rather fragile, element of support for the disrupted right flank of Villeroi's army, at a time when the Marshal had no idea that things were going wrong so badly in the south: 'I gradually rallied my grenadiers and several companies of the Cologne Regiment, making in all four small battalions, very much shaken.' The Colonel comments on this with some pride, several times driving off Dutch attempts to dislodge his men, but he exaggerates the importance of this well-intentioned, but entirely peripheral, operation, as the Dutch Guards found that they could just shoulder aside his small detachment, leaving them to languish beside the Visoule stream, as the vast, surging cavalry battle roared away across the open plain leading northwards to Ramillies village.

The complete failure of the inept French counterattack on the Dutch Guards in Franqenay and Taviers left the cavalry of their right Wing, already struggling to cover adequately the frontage allotted to them, now much weakened by the wasteful destruction of the fourteen squadrons of dragoons, and the ruin both of four Swiss battalions of infantry and of the Bavarian brigade. The two villages had been lost and the flank exposed and nothing achieved in return; almost without effort, the French had got off to a very poor start in the battle on the plain at Ramillies, and their cavalry was put at yet a further disadvantage. Richard Kane wrote afterwards, underlining the tactical difficulty that de Guiscard now faced in the wake of the fiasco in this important area: 'The intent of their interlining Foot with their Horse in the Plain, was to sustain the Horse in case of a Repulse, under the Shelter of whose fire they might easily rally again; for the Horse never care to come within the Fire of the Foot.' The failure on their right flank would, it must be assumed, have been attended to by the French commanders in time – it was certainly no minor matter. However, time was something that Villeroi and his generals did not have, and de Guiscard very soon had more pressing demands on his attention.

Meanwhile, at the other end of the wide battlefield, the British infantry commanded by George Hamilton, 1st Earl Orkney, were formed up in two lines of battle on the ridge-line opposite the valley of the Petite Gheete stream, beyond which were the barricaded villages of Offuz and Autre-Eglise. Around these cottages stood French, Bavarian and Walloon infantry, well posted in the gardens and orchards and backed by strong reserves of the Elector's Bavarian and Walloon cavalry on the plateau of Mont St André. At about 2.30 p.m. the first line of British infantry, who had been lying down to gain shelter from Villeroi's artillery and to rest in the hot sun, rose to their feet. Quickly picking up their dressing and, with colours flying bravely and to the tapping of the side-drums, they began the slow descent into the valley to their front, under the immediate command of the Earl, who went forward with the troops on foot. The second-line British battalions, now supported by six battalions of Danish infantry that came up in support, remained as observers on the ridge-line at the edge of the plateau of Jandrenouille.

The bramble thickets that littered the gentle slope of the

Autre-Eglise. The ridge-line seen from the British forming-up position.

De la Guiche's Walloon infantry

The Petite Gheete stream valley, seen from the edge of Offuz. The view that the Walloon infantry had of the British advance.

valley of the Petite Gheete were infested with Walloon outposts and sharpshooters, and these were cleared out, at some cost, with the bayonet. In the valley bottom, the pace of the soldiers slowed as they struggled through the boggy stream, and were met there with hedged bayonets and well-directed volleys of musketry from a brigade of tough infantry sent forward from around Offuz by Major General de la Guiche, to dispute their passage.

Tom Kitcher, a Hampshire farm labourer who had enlisted to serve with Meredith's Regiment, remembered pioneers laying fascines to ease their passage over the wet ground, and, as the regiment formed part of the second line in the advance, being unable to avoid trampling on the bodies of his fallen comrades as he struggled through the mud: 'Many were shot and maimed, or killed, by the French outposts.' The opposing brigade at the stream's edge were, actually, Walloons, and they did not stand their ground for long; the aim had been just to extract a suitably heavy price from the British for getting over the marsh, not to engage in an expensive and almost certainly doomed battle in the valley bottom against superior numbers. So de la Guiche's troops fell back up the slope in good order, a difficult manoeuvre when in close contact, which they accomplished with great skill, although Kitcher (who plainly made no distinction between the Walloons and their allies when referring to his enemies) recalled that 'I spiked one of the Frenchies through the gullet, and another through the arse where he spun like bacon upon a spit.' Forming their ranks again on the drier ground, the British infantry pressed up the slope under a heavy fire, and began to break through the hastily erected barricades around the cottages: 'I think I never had more shot around my ears', according to Orkney. Ferguson's Cameronians forced their way into Autre-Eglise a little to the north, but were promptly driven back out again at point of bayonet by the Régiment du Roi. This action, in fact, seems to have been a rather brief affair, as Major Blackader (or Blackadder) of that regiment remembered having very little to do all afternoon. The tough and well-led defenders on the ridge comfortably outnumbered Orkney's attacking infantry, but such was the

Autre-Eglise seen from across the Petite Gheete stream valley. De la Guiche's infantry held the far ridge-line.

De la Guiche's Walloon infantry

Marlborough's British troops advancing

Major John Blackad(d)er. His regiment, the Cameronians, were driven back out of Autre-Eglise by the Régiment du Roi.

vigour of the British assault, that it seemed that they would break right through the line of villages and out onto the open plateau of Mont St André. Here, unless adequate Allied cavalry came speedily forward across the difficult ground of the Petite Gheete valley to support them, the soldiers would be at the mercy of the Elector's Bavarian and Walloon squadrons, ideally placed and patiently waiting for the moment to move forward and ride down the British infantry, disordered, hot and weary after their hard fight to claim their place on the Ramillies–Offuz–Autre-Eglise ridge-line.

Orkney wrote afterwards that 'the village of Autre-Eglise was in our grip, but as I was going to take possession I had ten aides de camp to [tell] me to come off.' Marlborough

George Hamilton, 1st Earl Orkney, who led British infantry attacks on Offuz and Autre-Eglise.

knew that his infantry attack on the right, for all their local, seductively attractive success, could not be properly sustained, while at the same time full support was being given to Overkirk and his cavalry in the south. If pressed too far, onto the plateau of Mont St André, a disaster for the British infantry could well happen at the hands of the Elector's cavalry. To make quite sure that Orkney understood the order to withdraw, an order the belligerent Earl might well find fit to ignore in the heat of action, Marlborough also sent William Cadogan, the Quartermaster General, to ensure that the thing was done. Heated words were exchanged between the two men, Orkney urging that his success, bought at the price of many of his soldiers' lives, be reinforced and pushed onwards, and he pointed furiously to the squadrons of Henry Lumley's British cavalry, even now picking their cautious way across the marshy ground to support the infantry effort. Cadogan insisted that the Duke's order stood, Orkney reluctantly gave the word, and his troops fell back down the slope, littered with the bloody wreckage of their attack, into the Petite Gheete valley, and back up the slope to their starting point on the edge of the plateau of Jandrenouille. 'It vexed me to retire,' Orkney said; 'however we did it very well and in good order, and whenever the French pressed upon us, with the battalion of [1st Foot] Guards and my own [regiment], I was always able to stand and make them retire.'

Once securely back on the ridge facing Offuz, the wider plan became more apparent to the British officers, for the second-line battalions, shielded from observation by their opponents by a slight fold in the ground, began moving off southwards towards the centre of the field to support the attacks on Ramillies in response to Marlborough's summons. These British and Danish battalions of the second line were commanded on the day by the Dutch Brigadier General van Pallandt, a valiant hard-fighting

72

Church spire

De la Guiche's infantry on ridge-line

Offuz seen from the valley of the Petite Gheete stream. The British infantry fought their way across these fields, driving Walloon infantry back to the ridge-line.

officer in whom Marlborough had the highest confidence. He reportedly ordered that the regimental colours be left in place at the edge of the plateau, to further give the impression that the troops were still standing there, in full strength and ready to renew the attack at the right moment.

Marlborough was now throwing his full weight onto his left, but Marshal Villeroi, by contrast, remained concerned at the security of his own left around Offuz and Autre-Eglise. He was still moving reserves of infantry away from the plain to the south of Ramillies, up onto the plateau of Mont St André where, unknown to him, the Allied effort was now coming to a halt. Richard Kane, a skilled tactician, wrote that 'without firing a shot he [Marlborough] obliged them to break the Dispositions in the Centre, where they had placed the greatest Dependence of the success of the Battle.' The infantry support for de Guiscard's cavalry was really getting thin, even before allowing for the wasteful destruction of the French dragoons, the Swiss and the Bavarian brigade in their failed attempt to retake Taviers. De La Colonie had earlier noticed that amongst their cavalry 'there were large intervals between the squadrons, and that their formations were disproportionately extended', while another French observer summed up the situation neatly when he wrote, 'Thus the whole weight of the battle fell upon the right wing of the army, where the troops of His Majesty's Household [cavalry] were placed.'

Fortified farmhouse on the edge of Offuz village.

Chapter 4

MILORD MARLBOROUGH WAS RID OVER

A S THE BRITISH INFANTRY attack against Offuz and Autre-Eglise was gathering pace, the Allied assault on Ramillies village went in under the direction of Marlborough's younger brother and General of Infantry, Charles Churchill: 'He ordered four brigades of foot to attack the village.' Under heavy French artillery fire, twelve battalions of Dutch infantry, commanded by Major Generals Schultz and Spaar, moved resolutely forward, supported by two brigades of Saxons under Count Schulemberg. A Scottish brigade in Dutch service led by the 2nd Duke of Argyll, and a small brigade comprising two battalions of Protestant Swiss (who had until then been posted just to the south of the village, in support of the Dutch cavalry) also moved into the attack. The highly disciplined French gunners lowered the muzzles of their pieces and switched from round-shot to canister as the range closed, and the attackers, soon losing the meagre protection afforded by the slight rise in the ground on the edge of the plateau of Jandrenouille, began to go down in scores with each salvo.

The village was strongly held, with twenty French and Bavarian infantry battalions, supported by Clare's émigré regiment of (Irish) dragoons and a small brigade of the Cologne Guards and Bavarian Guards under the Marquis de Maffei. The garrison were seasoned troops, despite rather dismissive comments by at least one French officer that they lacked experience and were 'foreign battalions and recruits'. Even if that were so (and there seems to be an element of excuse-making, after the event, for the dire outcome of the day), they put up a tough and spirited

John Campbell,
2nd Duke of Argyll, 1st Duke of Greenwich (1678–1743)

The Duke of Argyll, whose grandfather, the 9th Earl, had been executed by King James II on account of his adherence to the Protestant religion, was commonly known as 'Red John' amongst the troops. John Campbell was an experienced soldier, having served, as Lord Lorne, in Flanders during the Williamite wars in the 1690s. At the siege of Venlo in 1702 he fought as a volunteer under 'Salamander' Cutts in the desperate storm of the citadel, and he commanded a brigade of Scots infantry, employed in the Dutch service, during the hectic assault on Ramillies village in May 1706. Argyll was reputed to have been one of the first of the attackers to step over the barricades at Ramillies, sword in hand, and was said to have been struck twice by spent musket balls, but was unharmed. He served under the Duke of Marlborough on many of his campaigns, but Argyll in time became an ardent critic of the Captain General, scorning his methods and questioning his motives, and was active in stirring up trouble for him in London.

In the latter phase of the Allied campaigns in Spain, Argyll was sent to command the British troops and was appalled at the corruption and inefficiency, most notably amongst Queen Anne's allies, that he found there. The soldiers were many months in arrears of pay, and Argyll had to use his own credit to see that they got enough money to avoid mutiny. The task he was given at this late stage was in fact impossible, but he acquitted himself well in the circumstances.

Argyll was also a noted and shrewd politician and had played an important role in the negotiations that led to the Union of Scotland and England in 1707. His antagonism towards Marlborough was shared by many, politicians and senior officers alike, as the War for Spain seemed to drag interminably on, but was remarkably ill-judged for such an otherwise shrewd man. His conduct was not forgotten by the Duke when, during the 1715 Jacobite rebellion, Marlborough (now reinstated by George I as Captain General) had Argyll removed from command of the government troops in Scotland, on the rather thin grounds that he was not energetic enough, replacing him with his own good friends, William Cadogan and then Joseph Sabine.

defence, driving back the attackers with heavy losses. Gallantly, the Dutch infantry renewed the attack and came on again, bayonets levelled, but they struggled forward in an absolute storm of musketry and canister fire, and were unable to make any impression at all on the defenders.

As the attacking infantry recoiled from the French barricades on the edge of Ramillies to recover their order, one of Argyll's Scottish battalions, Borthwick's, was driven back in such disorder by the French Régiment de Picardie, that the ensign carrying the regimental colour, James Gardiner, was shot in the mouth, and left for dead alongside the churchyard wall (he survived the dreadful wound and was killed at the head of his regiment of dragoons at Prestonpans thirty-nine years later). The colour, treasured symbol of regimental pride, was lost to a French soldier, and was only recovered after a bitter and murderous hand-to-hand fight in a sloping field of rye next to the church, in which the grenadier company of Collyer's Regiment also became engaged before the French could be driven back. The soldiers, both French and Scots, suffered heavy casualties in the fierce contest, with bayonets and clubbed muskets being freely used and their dead and wounded lying in thick droves, in their greyish-white and red coats, along the lanes and hedges around the churchyard. Despite this, the French grip on the village was, for the time being, unshaken.

Seeing that Schultz and Spaar were faltering with the assault on Ramillies, with every prospect, in fact, that their attack would fail completely, Marlborough sent for a brigade of Orkney's reserve infantry, now standing on the ridge overlooking the Petite Gheete stream, to add weight to the flagging effort. These troops had not gone in to the attack on Offuz and Autre-Eglise, although Orkney would, in other circumstances, have called them forward before too long, to provide the essential second echelon to move through and exploit the Earl's hard-won success. The three battalions (Churchill's, McArtney's and Mordaunt's) were now brought to the centre of the field to support the attack there, and others would follow. Robert Parker saw the move and remembered that, 'As soon as our rear line had retired out of sight of the enemy, they immediately formed to the left, and both horse and foot, with a good many squadrons, that slunk out of the front line, marched down to the plain, as fast as they could.'

This began a subtle and powerful shift in emphasis by the Duke, as he drew more and more troops to his left, and the weight of the attacks grew in the south and correspondingly lessened in the north. The escalating cavalry battle in the south, and the opportunity presented by the glaringly exposed right flank of the French and Bavarian army, required Orkney to call off his own attack against Offuz and Autre-Eglise. Crucially, it would be some time before Villeroi appreciated that vital change in emphasis in the Duke's effort, and whether he could respond in time to the new unfolding threat to his right, as he simultaneously reinforced his own left, remained to be seen.

At about 3.30 p.m., while the Allied infantry attacks, in their centre and on the right, ground steadily forward, Veldt Marshal Overkirk led his forty-eight squadrons of Dutch cavalry onto the open plain to the south of Ramillies. They were supported on their left by the twenty-one Danish squadrons who had already taken up a position beside Taviers. The massed squadrons advanced at a steady pace, care was taken not to tire the horses prematurely that hot afternoon, and Colonel De La Colonie remembered that the Dutch cavalry seemed 'like solid walls, while we had but three lines, the third of which was composed of several squadrons of dragoons.' This technique, used to such good effect by the Allied cavalry that afternoon, was known at the time as riding 'en muraille', and involved the troopers keeping well closed up, knee to knee in formation, with arms

The Decision-Making Cycle

All commanders seek to mislead their opponents about their own intentions – that is common sense. It is also necessary to find out what an opponent intends to do, and to take steps in good time to foil those intentions, as far as possible, in the time available. The really successful general will also strive to get inside his opponent's decision-making cycle which, in simple terms, is achieved by making good decisions, and implementing those decisions, faster than the opponent can do. Given a general equality of opposing troop strengths, their training, morale and weapon capabilities (spears will rarely succeed against machine guns, for instance), the commander who in this way successfully operates inside his opponent's decision-making cycle will win, with almost mathematical certainty. The less alert opponent, outside the decision-making cycle of the more active commander, will always be reacting to the other's moves, and have no time to implement his own decisions, which may, in their own way, be perfectly good but not able ever to be put into practice.

This simple concept, which is enormously demanding in practice, was clearly put to excellent use by Marlborough at Ramillies. The two armies, in broadly equal strengths, had closed up to each other by noon on 23 May 1706. The Duke then began a series of rapid, highly competent movements which led to him switching the main effort from the infantry attacks on his right to the cavalry battle on the left. This decision can only have been taken while the battle was in progress, and the French commander's reinforcement of his left, in response to the Duke's own infantry attacks, had become evident. Marshal Villeroi, at this point in the mid-afternoon, was so impressed by the Allied infantry attacks in the north that he was stripping supports away from his cavalry in the south, which had by then become, unknown to him, the focal point for Marlborough's main assault. When this unfolding danger became clear to Villeroi, as it certainly did, the Marshal had no time to properly rearrange the deployment of his army to meet the crushing cavalry attack that destroyed his right Wing and swept his army away in abject and panic-stricken flight.

outstretched and swords thrust forward; coming on at a gentle trot, gradually increasing speed until the moment of impact. The squadrons meeting a charge performed in this highly disciplined way would, unless they were led forward by their commanders in a similar resolute fashion to meet it with full vigour, literally be overthrown and driven back. 'I now saw the enemy's cavalry squadrons advance', De La Colonie wrote. 'The Maison du Roi decided to meet them, for at such a moment those who await the shock find themselves at a disadvantage.' The Dutch, able to deploy superior numbers in the first line, had an obvious advantage, regardless of whether de Guiscard's squadron commanders could properly employ the same masterful technique.

The ability of Overkirk to mass his full strength in this initial attack, in contrast to the French arrangements, was also commented on by the Marquis de Feuquières, in a journal written after the battle, which describes the 'en muraille' technique used rather well:

> *They advanced in four lines to our right wing of cavalry ... As they approached they advanced their second and fourth lines into the intervals of their first and third lines; so that when they made their advance upon us, they formed only one front, without any intermediate spaces. This motion was performed so near us, that our right had no time either to close themselves, in order to fill the intervals by that contraction, or to supply* [reinforce] *them with the second line, which, beside their immoderate distance from the first line, were incapable of making that advance on account of the several equipages left, through mere negligence, between the two lines.*

Despite all this, given the struggle that Overkirk's horsemen would have in the smoke and dust before the day was over, the valour of the French cavalry is not in any doubt. It was their lack of numbers, made even worse by Villeroi stripping away the important reserves of infantry in his absorbing concern for his left flank, that would become the telling handicap as the afternoon and evening wore on. Such a drastic structural tactical disadvantage defies bravery and energy in putting to rights.

Now that lack of support for the French squadrons required to cover the frontage adequately, engineered by the French commander in so assiduously reinforcing his left, made its presence felt most forcefully. The French first-

Cavalry combat at Ramillies. Oil sketch by Louis Laguerre. Courtesy of the Marquess of Anglesey.

line cavalry responded magnificently to the Dutch and Danish advance and came forward to meet them with great dash, but their squadrons were soon thrown into disorder and driven back by superior numbers of Dutch and Danes. They retired upon the support of the second-line squadrons to recover their order and rest their horses, but this French second line was almost immediately under pressure too, and had to retire on the inadequate third line and the few infantry battalions remaining on the plain. Still, de Guiscard's troopers recovered their order, and 'here the cavalry charged each other for a considerable time, with various success', Richard Kane wrote afterwards, 'the Foot on both sides often stopping the squadrons in their career.' The troops fought with valour and tenacity, and whatever advantage was gained from time to time was dearly bought. Captain Robert Parker remembered that 'sometimes their squadrons and sometimes ours gave way in different places; and as the fate of the day depended entirely on the behaviour of the troops on the plain [to the south of Ramillies] so both sides exerted themselves with vigour for a long time.'

These cavalry were the best the French had, superbly mounted and well-trained elite squadrons of the Maison du Roi, the Household cavalry – the Gardes du Corps, the Royal Carabiniers, the Mousquetaires, the Grenadiers à Cheval and the Gens d'Armes, supported by four elite squadrons of Bavarian cuirassiers, 'riding closen liken to a brassen wall', as an observer remembered. All were under the superb leadership of de Guiscard, who exerted himself in positions of the greatest peril that long afternoon, and they rallied more than once and returned to the attack with whirling and slashing swords, thrusting back the Dutch squadrons in forthright and quite unexpectedly successful local counterattacks. This day there were no time-consuming pauses to fire off pistols and carbines (as so often handicapped the French troopers at this period), and on Overkirk's right flank, quite close to Ramillies, ten of his squadrons suddenly broke ranks and were scattered, riding headlong to the rear to recover their order. A crisis threatened in the centre as the Dutch cavalry here gave way, exposing the left flank of the Swiss and German infantry brigades trying to break into Ramillies village. A brief chance appeared to offer for de Guiscard to throw his cavalry forward with all its might and split the Allied army in two. The threat was real enough, and de Guiscard at the head of massed cavalry in a headlong charge was a formidable proposition. However, although Marlborough could not yet know this, the French squadrons did not have sufficient strength by this time to make their blow really count.

The Duke was nearby, anxiously watching the progress of the milling cavalry battle, well aware that the day was not yet won. He had just given orders for eighteen squadrons of Dutch cavalry, held back in reserve near Ramillies, to move to Overkirk's assistance, and he now called for all the cavalry of his right Wing, except the British squadrons under Henry Lumley who remained in support of Orkney's infantry attacks, to come southwards also. While he waited for the fresh squadrons to travel the short distance over the fields of wheat and get into position, the Duke was almost alone, with just a couple of aides and his trumpeter in attendance, when the French squadrons suddenly came surging towards his party. Marlborough turned and spurred towards Murray's Swiss brigade, which stood a few hundred yards away, but in the confused press of riders, his horse stumbled at a ditch and the Duke was thrown heavily to the ground. The French could not mistake the Captain General, a conspicuous figure in his faded red coat and garter sash. 'They fired their long pistols' and dashed forward to hack him down. 'Milord Marlborough', Orkney wrote later, 'was rid over.'

Marlborough's custom was to wear comfortable linen gaiters, rather than the more common high-boots, and on this occasion they served him well. Scrambling to his feet, with an agility that did credit to a fifty-six-year-old man just thrown from his horse, the Duke ran towards the nearby Swiss brigade, closely pursued by sword-swinging French horsemen. A British officer remembered that 'the Duke when he got to his feet again saw Major General Murray coming up and ran directly to get in to his battalions.' It was a race for his life, a race that the Duke narrowly won, finding shelter in the disciplined ranks of the Swiss soldiers who then threw back the pursuing troopers, some of whom had been so close that their horses careered on and were impaled on the bayonets. Murray offered Marlborough his own horse, but his aide-de-camp, Captain Robert Molesworth, hastily led up one of the Duke's own remounts, and he was soon back in the saddle, rather bruised and a little breathless from the escapade, but otherwise unharmed. After the slightest pause,

Louis-Joseph de Bourbon, Duc de Vendôme. Succeeded Villeroi as army commander after Ramillies.

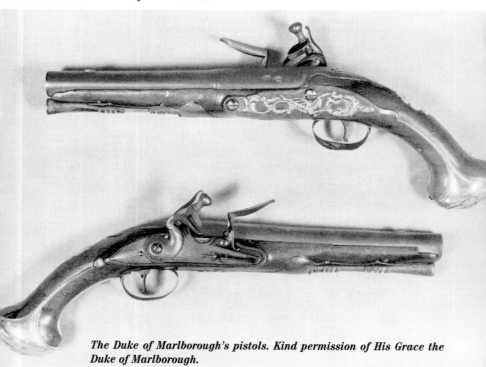

The Duke of Marlborough's pistols. Kind permission of His Grace the Duke of Marlborough.

Marlborough could look around and attend to the positioning of the cavalry reinforcements feeding down from the north of the field in increasing numbers. Their arrival to the south of Ramillies accomplished the dramatic shift in the tactical balance on the battlefield, a shift of which Marshal Villeroi was still blissfully unaware.

Soon afterwards, as the Duke changed horses once again, a French round-shot, fired from a battery on the edge of Ramillies, neatly decapitated Colonel James Bringfield, his aide, who was helping the Duke into the saddle. 'Bringfield, holding his stirrup to give him another horse, was shot with a cannon ball, which went through Marlborough's legs. In truth there was no scarcity of them', Orkney remembered. The unfortunate colonel's headless body, fountaining blood, fell to the ground at Marlborough's feet, an episode that was commemorated in a remarkably lurid set of playing cards that subsequently enjoyed great popularity in England. 'The ball took off Major Brinfeilde's head just by my Lord Duke's side', wrote John Deane of the 1st English Foot Guards.

Serving as a staff officer to the Duke was plainly no quiet sinecure, and young Robert Molesworth who, almost alone of his aides, had been with him in the dash to the shelter of Murray's brigade, was almost hacked down in the mêlée around the hedged bayonets of the Swiss infantry square, quite apart from his being in danger of being shot down by his own troops: 'the Captain, being immediately after[wards] surrounded by the enemy, from which danger (as well as from our own fire) he was, at last, providentially delivered.' The time was about 4.30 p.m., and the two armies were in close contact across the whole four-mile-wide battlefield, from the grubby skirmishing in the marshes of the Visoule stream in the south, through the vast cavalry battle on the open plain, to the desperate infantry battles for Ramillies in the centre and at Offuz and in Autre-Eglise to the north, where the soldiers of Orkney

The Battle of Ramillies where y D of Marlbo
roug &c: took 26, Standards & 63, Enfigns the
French loosing 20000, men all their Baggage
Amunition &c.

*Contemporary playing card, depicting the decapitation of Bringfield by a
French round-shot while helping Marlborough to mount his horse.*

and de la Guiche faced each other across the Petite Gheete
stream, ready for a fresh onset of the battle. Villeroi was off
balance, and this uncomfortable fact should now have been
dawning on him, as the Allied cavalry deployment in the
south grew in strength and reached out around his flank.
The French and Bavarian army was fixed tactically; it was
fighting well, but fighting for its life. Marlborough alone
retained the initiative, and the next moves were entirely in
his hands.

Chapter 5

SAVE YOURSELVES IF YOU CAN

*T*HE VALIANT FRENCH CAVALRY, for all their efforts, were gradually being worn down in the battle on the plain to the south of Ramillies. Richard Kane remembered that 'the Household Troops [French cavalry] who had hitherto behaved with great Bravery, rallied and came again to the Charge; but the French Fire [spirit] which on all first onsets seemed very furious, was now spent.' They had, from the very start, struggled to adequately cover the frontage allotted to them, and the rapidly growing list of casualties inexorably added to their problem; the French squadrons shrank in size and as they did so, the frontage they could cover shrank too. General de Guiscard's cavalry were becoming tired, and their numerical inferiority was telling at last, as Veldt Marshal Overkirk's troopers found that they could thread through the wide intervals between their squadrons, engage them from the flank, and even, on occasions, hack at the French troopers from the rear. The Marquis de Feuquières recalled that:

> *They* [the Dutch] *wheeled about to charge the squadrons of our first line from the rear who, after they had almost defeated all the squadrons that attacked them, were now thrown into a general disorder by the squadrons of the enemy's second line, and by those who charged them in the rear.*

The French cavalry could not fall back on the protection of their infantry supports to catch their breath, recover their order and rest the horses before a fresh effort, unlike their more fortunate opponents.

By late afternoon, as the losses amongst the French

squadrons mounted, the fatal gap had opened wider on the right of their line, where the early, uncorrected, failure to hold or retake Franquenay and Taviers had already exposed their flank. Into this gap Colonel Wertmüller's Dutch Guards had been thrust, and they were soon supported by Dopff's, Holstein's and Opdham's regiments of dismounted dragoons. With this powerful support, the squadrons of the Duke of Württemberg's Danish cavalry had slipped through, right past the flank of de Guiscard's horsemen, whose attention was almost entirely fixed by now on holding back the Dutch cavalry attack. Virtually without any hindrance, apart from some fugitive remnants of the French dragoons who had been dispersed earlier in the afternoon (many of whose untended horses managed to find the way unaided to their own stables twenty or so miles away), the twenty-one Danish squadrons formed up in the area of the tomb of Ottomonde. They turned to face northwards across the trampled wheat of the wide plain to Ramillies and the plateau of Mont St André beyond, where the equipages (as the Marquis de Feuquières put it), the baggage and tentage of the French army, still lay carelessly lying about.

As early evening came on, there was a short pause in the pace of fighting across the wide battlefield, as the Allied army, ideally placed to deliver its blow, caught its collective breath, and readied itself for the great effort. Their French, Walloon and Bavarian opponents, by comparison, were grateful for the brief chance to try and recover their order. Weariness was playing its part, certainly in the south where the French squadrons could hardly raise their blown horses to the pace of a gentle trot, and aides were now hurrying northwards to find Marshal Villeroi, and urge that assistance be sent from the ample reserves held back behind the villages. Their Dutch opponents, after a hectic afternoon, were not much better off, although these squadrons retained still the advantage in proper infantry

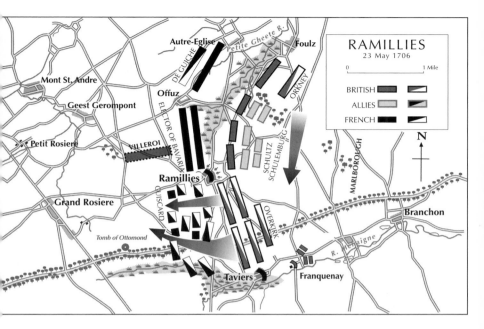

Ramillies, attack phase 2.

support, and the Danish cavalry nearby were comparatively fresh.

In the centre of the field, the opposing infantry stared at each other over the bloody barricades in and around Ramillies, the dead and wounded lying thickly scattered around. The garrison of the village, all but irrelevant now to the wider battle, were battered but still firmly in possession, while the attackers, Dutch, Swiss, German and British, gathered their strength for another attack. On the ridge-lines to the north, Earl Orkney's contingent of British troops, horse and foot, looked across the Petite Gheete valley at de la Guiche's infantry and the Elector of Bavaria's massed cavalry. Still standing behind Offuz and Autre-Eglise, they had as yet played no really active part in the battle. According to Richard Kane, 'their left Wing and the Front Line of our Right, where our Regiment was, stood looking on all the while without striking a stroke.' So time that was vital to Villeroi in reordering his army and getting fresh troops into the right position to meet the unfolding threat to his right Wing, was allowed to go to waste, while for Marlborough, this period of inactivity simply added to the chances for his success off to the south. The longer he could keep Villeroi's attention occupied in the north, the better the chance of success. The final reinforcements for the cavalry contest in the south had now moved into position at Marlborough's direction, and the only movement of real note across the whole four miles of battlefield at this point was in the calm ordering of the ranks of the Danish cavalry near the tomb of Ottomonde, looking with grim anticipation towards the exposed flank of Villeroi's army. The Marshal was now dreadfully out of position, held in place by the combination of Marlborough's concurrent brutal attacks and bewildering shifts in emphasis throughout the afternoon.

The Danish cavalry movement clear around the right flank of the French army had not gone by any means unnoticed; such a substantial body of horsemen would be very visible in open country such as this, even at a distance of a mile or so. As it was, Villeroi may have felt, until this point, that he had fought rather a good battle; the Allied infantry attacks had been held or bloodily thrown back, while Overkirk's Dutch squadrons had been roughly handled and mauled by de Guiscard's troopers in their fight in the south of the battlefield. Furthermore, the Marshal had plenty of reserves, both cavalry and infantry, in good order and ready to hand behind Ramillies and Offuz. Now, suddenly and shockingly, he was brought to realize that the loss of Taviers and Franquenay, to which no proper attention had been given or effort made to recapture, had fatally exposed his army to a flank attack in crushing force, a blow that he could not hope now to counter with some late rearrangement of his troops. His opponent had massed cavalry in overwhelming strength on a part of the field that was simply too far away for Villeroi to redeploy his reserves in good time to meet the threat. The Marshal was off-balance, merely reacting to Marlborough's skilled moves on the battlefield, with no real chance of recovery. It was all too late.

The resilience and cohesion of the French right Wing was very fragile after their efforts and, increasingly, men began to glance behind them, disregarding the shouted orders and entreaties of their officers, seeking an avenue of escape from what was fast looking like a trap. At about 6 p.m. Villeroi and the Elector of Bavaria, having ridden hastily over to Ramillies from their watch over de la Guiche's infantry around Offuz and Autre-Eglise, found that fugitives were streaming past them, heading for the roads that led to the north and west. Urgently, the two commanders began to draw out from the plateau of Mont St André the reserves of cavalry and infantry held in idleness there, and tried desperately to form a new line facing to the south, bent back at right angles to the original dispositions that were now of so little relevance to the survival of their army as a fighting force. Peter Drake wrote that his regiment, de Courrière's, 'was ordered on [towards Ramillies] and having got within pistol shot, we were commanded to face to the right about and retire.' The baggage, wagons and tentage, so neglectfully left lying around in the area behind Ramillies, inevitably hampered the attempted reordering of the left Wing of the army, but it was probably too late anyway, as the irresistible dynamics of Marlborough's fast-unfolding plan took hold of the battlefield.

Neither side had an obvious advantage across the centre and north of the battlefield where the opposing batteries still hammered away at each other. Only Marlborough retained the initiative now, for his cavalry, the Dutch and the Danes in the south, were about to deliver a death blow to the French and Bavarian army, and Marshal Villeroi, for all his competent arrangements and recent energy, could only watch it happen – nothing he attempted would take effect before Marlborough's awful cavalry stroke went in against the right Wing of his army. Near the Tomb of Ottomonde, meanwhile, nothing was rushed, although a stunning victory, of unimaginable scale, beckoned the Allied commanders; nothing was to be thrown away by rashness or mismanagement. The dressing and alignment of Württemberg's Danes and Overkirk's Dutch, their horses standing in a great arc from just south of Ramillies to the hamlet of Ottomonde, was checked, the barked commands of officers and NCOs mingling with the groans and pleadings of the wounded lying scattered around on the trampled cornfield. The Duke of Marlborough had now joined the Veldt Marshal, and at the word of command this vast imposing array of horsemen surged forward against the outnumbered and weary French squadrons. 'Up comes the Danish Duke of Wirtemberg with the Danish Horse', Richard Kane wrote, 'also falling on their flank ... [and] charg'd them with such a fury that it put them into great disorder.' Even with the French and Bavarian squadrons that were being scrambled together by Villeroi in an attempt to form a new line of battle that would hold the Allied onslaught, de Guiscard's cavalry could not resist the new attack. Turning their horses' heads to the northwards, the exhausted cavalry of the French right Wing broke ranks and fled from the field in wild disorder, trampling down anyone – foot-soldier, cannoneer, servant or camp follower – who got in the way.

Villeroi's army, which just half an hour before had been fighting well and in good order, now fled for their lives. 'The cry went up', Peter Drake remembered, 'Sauve qui Peut! Then might be seen whole brigades running together.' In moments, what had been a huge disciplined body of soldiers dissolved into a frantic mob. 'The Elector and

Alessandro, Marquis de Maffei. He commanded a German brigade in defence of Ramillies and La Haute Censée farm. Taken prisoner by Dutch cavalry.

La Haute Censée farm in Ramillies village, held by Maffei's German brigade.

Villeroi did all that was possible to keep them from breaking', Captain Robert Parker recalled, 'but our troops stuck so close to them, that they were put to the rout.'

In Ramillies village the Allied infantry at last broke through the defences in a renewed attack, the Duke of Argyll being amongst the first to clamber over the barricades, and the garrison was driven out at bayonet point. The Régiment de Picardie stood their ground and were caught between Borthwick's (now re-formed) Scots–Dutch regiment and part of the fresh British brigade brought down by Marlborough from the north. Colonel Borthwick was amongst those killed in the battle here, as was Charles O'Brien, the exiled Irish Viscount Clare, now in the French service, fighting at the head of his regiment of dismounted dragoons, when 'engaged with a Scotch regiment [Collyer's] between whom there was a great slaughter.' The Bavarian Grenadiers, who had been moved to the southern edge of the village as the threat developed on the plain, were routed and driven in confusion back through Ramillies by Spaar's Dutch infantry. They rallied with the small German brigade, composed of two battalions of the Cologne Guards and the Bavarian Guards, under the command of Alessandro Maffei. He vainly attempted to make a stand from a good position in the shelter of a sunken lane that runs from the village onto the plateau of Mont St André, and managed to get some companies of infantry back into nearby Haute Censée farm, which had recently been abandoned. Their musketry held the Allied infantry back for a short while. In this way, Maffei hoped to provide an anchor of a sort for the disordered French cavalry on the plain, upon which they could recover and fight back. It all proved in vain, as the Marquis rather drily remembered in his journal:

> *I then saw coming towards us a line of hostile cavalry; but as this cavalry was coming from the side from which I naturally had expected our own to arrive, I thought at first they must be our people ... I did not notice the green cockade they wore in their hats* [the Allied field recognition symbol] *which was indeed so small that it could hardly have been discerned at the distance ... I went towards the nearest of these squadrons to instruct their officer, but instead of being listened to was immediately surrounded and called upon to ask for quarter.*

Maffei was taken away by the Dutch cavalry, and his brigade soon afterwards joined in the flight from the battlefield, but they got entangled in the marshy ground at the head of the Petite Gheete stream, and mostly became prisoners of the advancing British infantry. The roads leading to the north and west away from the battlefield

The British cavalry charge and break the Elector of Bavaria's squadrons.
(Artist: R Caton Woodville)

were, in any case, choked with fugitives, and the sunken lanes which are such a feature of the area quickly became blocked with abandoned wagons and carts, adding to the appalling congestion. The Allied cavalry followed close behind, cutting and slashing amongst the fleeing soldiers. The pursuit by the Danish horsemen was particularly savage, as news had recently come in that numbers of their countrymen had been massacred after surrendering at the battle of Calcinato in northern Italy in April, and the cry for revenge was on everyone's lips. 'The flight' of Villeroi's army, de Feuquières wrote, 'became universal.'

Orkney, despite the smoke hanging about on the northern end of the field, could make all this out from the ridge-line to which his infantry had withdrawn a little earlier, after being brought back from their attacks on Offuz and Autre-Eglise. The right and centre of the French army was plainly in chaos, as were the rear areas of their army. The Earl did not wait for fresh orders, but sent his British troops back across the Petite Gheete stream to storm their triumphant way into Offuz, where de la Guiche's infantry had begun to melt away in the confusion of the evening. Seven squadrons of the Bavarian Horse Grenadiers and the Electoral Guards promptly moved forward from the plateau of Mont St André to block the advance, but were driven off with well aimed volleys of musketry from Orkney's leading battalions.

On the right of the British infantry, Hay's and Ross's regiments of dragoons picked their way across the difficult ground of the stream and, taking the rare chance to charge at full tilt, put to flight the Régiment du Roi, as this elite infantry unit hurriedly withdrew from Autre-Eglise. 'Our dragoons', John Deane wrote, 'pushing into the village of Autre-Eglise made a terrible slaughter of the enemy.' The French soldiers had paused to recover the knapsacks they had dumped on the ground when moving forward earlier in the day; now, they were ridden down and dispersed by the charging dragoons. Peter Drake recalled that they 'lay down their arms like poltroons, and surrendered themselves prisoners of war.' The Bavarian Horse Grenadiers and the Electoral Guards had withdrawn a little way after being driven off by the British infantry, and they formed a shield about the Elector and Villeroi, and tried to present a properly formed front as the British cavalry surged forward. They were charged by Henry Lumley's squadrons, 'à la hussarde, sword in hand, at a gallop', near Autre-Eglise, and scattered, as were the Spanish (Walloon) Guards nearby, their commander, the Marquis de Guertiere, being taken captive. This left the British cavalry free to move on and drive a wedge into the flank of the seething mass of fugitives as they streamed away from the battlefield. One of their commanders, Lieutenant General Cornelius Wood, saw both Marshal Villeroi and the Elector nearby in the press of fugitives but, not recognizing them in the fading twilight, he turned aside to secure some other senior French officers captive. 'Had I been so fortunate to have known, I had strained Corialinus [his horse] on whom I rode all the day of the battle to have made them prisoners.' The Queen's Regiment of Horse did, however, seize the well-known negro kettle-drummer of the Bavarian Electoral Guards; some reports say that the drummer was mortally wounded in the process, others that he was immediately taken into Queen Anne's service.

Amongst the cavalry and dragoons engaged on this flank was the intrepid Irish female soldier Christian Davies (or Walsh/Welsh), who had followed her husband to war by successfully masquerading as a man in the ranks of Hay's Dragoons. Now her illicit career as a warrior (one which she obviously greatly relished) came to an abrupt end, as she recalled, 'An unlucky shell from a [church] steeple struck the back part of my head and fractured my skull.' Too stunned to conceal her sex from the surgeon who tended her, Davies was dismissed from the regiment, but on

Marlborough receives the captured standards of Villeroi's broken army. (Artist: H Dupray)

account of her good character when serving as a soldier was allowed to serve on with the army as a sutleress to the war's end.

Although a number of French and Bavarian battalions gamely attempted to make a stand and staunch the flood of the Allied onslaught, the furious pace of Marlborough's pursuit could not be resisted for long. The Duc de St Simon wrote, 'Our retreat commenced in good order, but soon the night came and threw us into disorder. The defile of Judoigne became so gorged with baggage and the wreckage of the artillery we had been able to save, that everything was taken from us there.' For the victors of the day, no orders could possibly be given by the Allied generals as the evening sped on; individual commanders just drove their troops forwards, allowing their beaten enemies no chance to recover. The Allied infantry soon could not keep up, so fast was the chase, but their cavalry were off the leash, with the Duke and his staff riding amongst the pursuers, heading through the gathering night for the crossing places over the Dyle river, beyond which Villeroi's fleeing army, even in its shattered state, might find shelter. Orkney wrote of the difficulty of gathering his infantry quickly enough to overtake the fugitives: 'If I could only have got up in time we should have taken eight or nine battalions ... All night we knew nothing of one another, and Mr Lumley and I had resolved to march straight to the Dyle to their Lines.' At last, several miles away to the north, Marlborough called a halt shortly after midnight near Meldert, closer to Louvain than to Ramillies, and, weary after nineteen hours in the saddle this eventful day, lay down to sleep on the grass in the corner of a field, sharing his cloak with the Dutch field deputy, Sicco van Goslinga. No one in his party was quite sure where they were by then, so hectic had been their pursuit of their broken opponents. 'In short', Jemmy Campbell, who had taken part in the attack on Ramillies village with Borthwick's Regiment,

Allied Casualties at Ramillies

The scale of Marlborough's victory on 23 May 1706, and the utter devastation inflicted on his opponent's fine army, was the wonder of the age. This sense of wonder was heightened when the rather modest scale of losses suffered by the Duke's army that day became known, especially when compared with the awful losses in the French and Bavarian ranks (so numerous were those, in fact, that they were never accurately or convincingly calculated, although glib phrases such as 'half the army ceased to exist' trip all too easily off the tongue and the pen). The following table of Allied losses was published in Amsterdam, shortly after the battle:

CAVALRY	KILLED	WOUNDED
Colonels	2	3
Lieutenant Colonels	0	3
Majors	4	3
Captains	10	24
Lieutenants, Subalterns and Cornets	18	73
Troopers	343	695
Horses*	990	352

*Plainly, large numbers of wounded horses would have been put out of their misery as incapable of being saved. For the wounded troopers, the same simple, grim sanction was not available.

INFANTRY	KILLED	WOUNDED
Colonels	3 *	3
Lieutenant Colonels	1	3
Majors	2	3
Captains	9	38
Lieutenants, Subalterns and Ensigns	33	159
Soldiers	641	1,590

*Including Prince of Hesse-Cassell.

TOTALS	KILLED	WOUNDED
Officers	82	312
Troopers and soldiers	984	2,285
All ranks	1,066	2,597

TOTAL CASUALTIES: **3,663 killed and wounded**

Casualties amongst the artillery train, and the engineer train, are apparently not given as a distinct item. The officers would also have held regimental rank, and would probably be reflected above, but it is not clear what casualties were suffered by the NCOs and soldiers serving the guns. It is inconceivable that there were no losses amongst these men in the heavy artillery duel that day, or in the civilian teamsters whose job it was to drag the guns into position, so they are either hidden in the totals given here or must be added as a conjectured figure.

wrote home, 'it is a most glorious victory.'

Colonel De La Colonie was still on the edge of the marshy Visoule stream to the west of Taviers, and was under no real pressure as the Allied pursuit rushed away to the north and west. He withdrew with the survivors of his battered brigade, and those dragoons and Swiss that had been gathered together, to the French-held fortress of Namur, which was reached the following morning. The governor, although quite astounded to receive the appalling news of such a crushing defeat for the French and Bavarian army, was sufficiently alert to send out working parties with teams of horses and drag off several of the abandoned artillery pieces that littered the quickly emptying battlefield.

Chapter 6

MORE LIKE A DREAM THAN THE TRUTH

𝕿HE IMBALANCE IN THE TALLY of the casualties at Ramillies is plain evidence of the scale of the victory for the Duke of Marlborough on the one hand, and the extent of the disaster for Marshal Villeroi on the other. The Allied army lost 1,066 killed and 2,597 wounded, an astonishingly light total (particularly when compared with the 5,041 who fell at the numerically smaller assault at the Schellenberg, or the 13,000 or more Allied casualties at Blenheim, nearly two years earlier). The French and Bavarian army at Ramillies, by stark comparison, suffered more than 12,000 killed and wounded – the precise total could never be calculated, so complete was the collapse of the army that day, and it was reported that another 10,000 unwounded prisoners were taken by the victors (John Millner, seventeen years after the battle, reckoned that 12,087 of Villeroi's men were killed or wounded, with another 9,729 taken prisoner or defected to the Allies). In addition, hundreds of French soldiers were fugitives, no longer with their units, and many of these would never remuster to the colours. The French and Bavarians lost fifty-two of the sixty artillery pieces they took into action, and their entire engineer pontoon train was left lying on the abandoned field of battle. Marlborough's army captured no less than eighty regimental colours, as well as almost all the campaign gear of the army, a vast haul of ammunition, materiel, camp stores, baggage and other booty. For a while, French and Bavarian soldiers in the Southern Netherlands were no more than fugitives.

In effect, it can be seen that well over a third of the

French and Bavarian army had ceased to exist, being casualties or prisoners, and the morale of the remainder was so shaken by the dreadful experience that Sunday that their effectiveness as a fighting force was in shreds. 'The most dreadful thing of all', wrote the Elector of Bavaria, shedding tears of shock, the day after the battle, 'is the terror that is in our troops.' Marlborough's army, on the other hand, had not only got off fairly lightly (although some units, particularly those engaged in the fighting for Taviers and the repeated attacks and counterattacks at Ramillies, had suffered quite heavily), but were buoyed up by their success and would soon receive substantial, long-awaited, contingents of fresh German troops, as reinforcements left their cantonments along the Rhine and hurried to join the campaign.

What was left of Villeroi's once fine army was now physically shattered, broken in spirit and engaged only in panic-stricken flight. That Sunday night, the Marshal and the Elector of Bavaria had met with those senior officers who had eluded Marlborough's cavalry, by torchlight, in the square of Louvain. There was widespread despair at the scale of their unprecedented defeat,

Commemorative medallion produced after Ramillies.

106

and no one believed the line of the Dyle could be held; possibly also the Senne river, the next practical line of defence, would be lost in the days ahead. Peter Drake remembered, 'We never halted until break of day, near Louvain where we crossed the river dispirited and weary, having been on our feet twenty-four hours without the least rest.' Instructions were immediately issued to set fire to the huge stocks of munitions and materiel gathered in the town, and dump what could not be burned into the river; Drake wrote that thousands of sacks of flour were destroyed in this way. Orders were given for what was left of the army to fall back to the line of the Dender river; there, perhaps, a stand might be made against the Allied onslaught that was sure to follow. So scattered were the French and Bavarians in the wake of defeat that fewer than 15,000 of Villeroi's army rallied to the colours in the days immediately after the battle. Almost all their artillery had been abandoned on the field and, in such a grossly weakened state, the Marshal could hope to do little more than to save what was left of his army, which, with better fortune, might live to fight Marlborough another day.

The sheer number of prisoners taken that hot day was rather an encumbrance for the Allied army as it moved forward, and Overkirk wrote to the States-General: 'I have given leave to many of my prisoners to go home, upon their parole, for three months; some of them being much wounded, and others having, by the Fate of War, been stripp'd of their cloathes.' The Veldt Marshal is presumably referring here to the officers rather than the ordinary soldiers, although it is quite possible that these gave parole for their men also. Marlborough, for all the pressing demands on his time, wrote a number of letters of instruction to his own officers concerning the accounting for and management of those taken captive. A couple of days later, his letter to Sir Richard Temple ran:

Understanding that there are a great many French

prisoners at Tirlemont, I desire you will remain there
with your regiment and take them under your care till
further orders. If you find any number of them in a
condition to march, I would have you send them with an
escort to Leau ... Pray let me have a list of the names and
qualities [rank] *of the officers you find there, with the*
numbers and conditions of the private men.

The letter announcing the extraordinary victory, sent by
Marlborough to his Duchess the day after the battle, read:

On Sunday last we fought and that God Almighty has
been pleased to give us a victory. I must leave the
particulars to the bearer, Colonel Richards, for having
been on horseback all Sunday, and after marching all
night, my head aches to the degree that it is very uneasy
to me to write. Poor Bringfield, holding my stirrup for
me, and helping me on horseback, was killed. I am told
that he leaves his wife and children in a poor condition.

Marlborough had ordered his victorious troops to close up
to the Dyle, heading to bridge the water obstacle with the
pontoon train of the army without delay. Coming
immediately after a tumultuous battle and headlong pursuit
through the night, this was a demanding logistical
operation, but the officers of Marlborough's engineer train
were equal to the task. By nightfall on Monday, 24 May the
Duke's troops were at the gates of Louvain, and the town
yielded the following day. Marlborough moved his
headquarters just to the north and, after a brief pause to
gather his troops and assess the likelihood of meeting
French resistance to his front, he lunged forward, his
cavalry columns taking several individual routes, each
commander seeking for the line of least resistance. In the
event, that resistance was really not there; Villeroi's fugitive
army was mostly concerned with drawing away from the
peril in which it stood. The French commanders were
walking through a waking nightmare, and those few
generals who had thoughts for anything other than flight to

Marlborough's Ramillies Dispatch

Sent to Queen Anne, 24 May 1706

Madam,

I humbly crave leave to congratulate Your Majesty with all humility and respect on the glorious success wherewith it pleased God yesterday to bless Y.M.'s arms and those of your allies over the enemy, who were equally desirous to come to a battle with us, having got together all their strength in these parts. I have been on horseback the whole day and last night, in order to press the enemy in their retreat, and am but just come to my quarters to send Colonel Richards to Y.M. with an account of this action, wherein all the troops, both officers and soldiers, have behaved themselves with the greatest bravery and courage, but I must humbly beg Y.M. will permit me to refer to the Colonel for the particulars. I hope the troops will be able to march again to-morrow night, in order to see if the intrenchments behind the Dyle may be attacked, having no greater pleasure than on all these occasions to show the sense I have of Y.M.'s great goodness to me.

I am, with the greatest devotion, Madam, etc. etc.

The Queen's reply, with a plain reference to Marlborough's mischievous opponents in London, ran:

I want words to express my true sense of the great service you have done to your country, and I hope it will be a means to confirm all good and honest men in their principles, and frighten others from being troublesome ... I must repeat my earnest request that you would be careful of yourself.

the fortress belt along the French border simply hoped to find a place where they could make a stand of some kind.

The Senne was reached and the Duke crossed that river near the chateau of Beaulieu on 26 May, from where the magistrates of Brussels, capital of the Spanish Netherlands, were summoned to surrender. Villeroi and his officers had ridden off, and the Governor of the city replied to Marlborough that day:

The States of Brabant and the Magistracy of Brussels, have taken the Resolution to send Deputies to you; they have desired me, Sir, to write to you, most humbly to desire you to send a Trumpeter, to conduct them in

Safety, to the Place where you shall think fit to receive them. I have not the Honour, Sir, to say more to you, concerning my Particular Interests, and those of the other Persons of Quality, who seem resolved to stay there, if you approve of it.

The hint to the Duke, rather heavily dropped, that the Governor was inclined to change sides, is quite plain. The keys to the city were ceremoniously handed to Marlborough on 28 May, and the States of Brabant did the same, the Duke assuring them, on behalf of Charles III, that their ancient rights and privileges, 'The Joyous Entry of Brabant', would be maintained. That this was not entirely to be the case in practice would be the cause of some trouble two years later in the prelude to the Oudenarde campaign.

It was plain to the Duke what a huge advantage he had gained so early in the campaign, and he wrote to Robert Harley on the day that Brussels fell: 'The consequence of the battle is likely to be of greater advantage than that of Blenheim; for we have now the whole summer before us, and with the blessing of God, I will make the best use of it.' He added, with plain reference to his past difficulties with the Dutch generals and deputies, 'We had no council of war before this battle, so I hope to have none this whole campaign.' The Duke's intention was clear: with the French in disarray and such glittering prospects ahead, Dutch caution, understandable as it might have been on earlier occasions, was not to be allowed to interfere with the decisions Marlborough now made. In fact, the field deputies (van Cotten, van Rheede, and van Goslinga), so often reluctant and overly careful in the past, were now almost beside themselves with glee at the triumph, writing to The Hague, also on the day that Brussels submitted to the Allies:

The Confusion the Enemy were in, after the Battle, cannot be expressed, as we are informed by the Seigneur de Gravenmoor, who was an Eye-Witness thereof ... in short, the Victory is complete and the happy Consequences thereof begin to appear.

Meanwhile, the Elector of Bavaria had written to Louis XIV with an account of the awful events on the field of Ramillies:

Your Majesty's household [cavalry] *and my cuirassiers broke no less than three times the enemy's left ... The only consolation, sir, in my misfortune, is, that I have done nothing contrary to your orders, which Marshal Villeroy cannot but acknowledge, as well as all the officers of the army, who have seen me expose myself as much as the meanest soldier; and if the peril of my life would have purchased a victory, it would assuredly not have been my fault, that your Majesty's army had not been triumphant.*

In Versailles the dreadful news of defeat from the Low Countries did not arrive until Wednesday 26 May and was greeted with incredulity. Rumours of a battle had arrived sooner, as Villeroi had thoughtfully written to a friend at Court that his son, although wounded in the action, was in no danger of his life. Matters were made worse by the arrival of messengers to announce that a French attempt to recapture Barcelona, recently stormed by the Allied army in Catalonia, had been successfully repulsed.

Now 'days seemed like years in the ignorance of everyone as to the details', according to St Simon. As the awful details came in, the King, 'forced to ask one and another for news, here and there', was reticent in his comments on the lamentable performance of Villeroi, his old friend, but many others stepped forward readily enough to denounce the Marshal's incompetence at Ramillies. Prominent amongst these was Michel de Chamillart, the War Minister, who had so recently urged Villeroi to go out and seek battle. Now de Chamillart was sent to Courtrai on 30 May, a week after the battle, to confer with the Marshal on what was to be done for the best. On the way he drew up a list of Villeroi's mistakes – he had sought battle without ascertaining his opponent's real strength; he had fought without waiting for full reinforcement from the army in the Moselle valley; he had failed to reinforce his right Wing, and (in close conjunction) he had placed insufficient infantry on the right; he had inefficiently deployed the right Wing in the battle, so that they had insufficient supports. De Chamillart was busily scheming to deflect any possible criticism from himself, of course; his erroneous judgement of Marlborough's performance in 1705 might yet come back to haunt him. His criticisms of the tactical failure on Villeroi's right flank, in particular, while correct, were so obviously reached with the useful benefit of hindsight that they were worth little comment. The first two considerations were plain nonsense – the War Minister was strident amongst those who had urged Villeroi on to battle that fateful Sunday, and, in fact, Villeroi had even been cautioned to wait for cavalry reinforcements from Marsin, which he had done, despite being impatiently urged by Versailles to get on with things.

Louis XIV was affronted by reports of how his Household cavalry, the Maison du Roi, had galloped off the field of battle in such indecent haste that Sunday, and eagerly seized for consolation upon anecdotes of individual bravery and gallant conduct. St Simon remembered that 'he sent word to the Guards that he was well contented with them, but others were not so easily satisfied', while Marshal Villars on the upper Rhine commented, on receipt of the news, that the French defeat in the battle was the most disgraceful thing he had ever heard. This judgement does less than justice to the French cavalry and their bravery, to their commander, General de Guiscard, whose performance that afternoon was selflessly valiant, and to the Duke of Marlborough, whose sparkling and dynamic tactics were so thoroughly successful.

In the meantime, Villeroi found it impossible to hold the line of the Dender against Marlborough's thrusting

The Magistrates of Oudenard wait
upon the D. of Marlboro desire his
protection & swear fidelity to K.C.y iij
June the 3. 1706.

Contemporary playing card, depicting the submission of the magistrates of Oudenarde to Marlborough after Ramillies.

columns, and attempted to establish a new position on the Scheldt, to cover Ghent and Bruges and the northern part of Flanders. Before he could manage this, however, Marlborough's advanced guard (twelve squadrons of cavalry and dragoons together with a picked force of 2,000 grenadiers), commanded by the Duke of Württemberg, had cut across the Marshal's right flank, passing the Scheldt at Gavre, just downstream from Oudenarde, on 31 May. That town capitulated shortly afterwards, and with his lines of communication and supply into France under threat, Villeroi had no choice but to abandon Ghent and Bruges. De Chamillart and the Marshal met at Courtrai on the Lys river, where their army, or what remained of it, fell back to recover their composure. Given the catastrophe that had been suffered, and that the French troops available in the Spanish Netherlands were in little condition to offer organized resistance to the Allied advance, de Chamillart approved Villeroi's plan to abandon the region and to withdraw to shelter inside the dense fortress belt along France's northern border. It was therefore necessary to disperse many regiments to occupy the various fortresses that now lay in Marlborough's path, and before long the French army had almost entirely gone into static defence. Only Mortagne, Armentières and Dendermonde were to be held as forward posts and, for the time being, the Duke of Marlborough was not faced with a French force capable of sustaining anything like a general action. Constrained only by logistics, he could do what he pleased.

Faced with the stark facts of the destruction at Ramillies of his army's operational ability, Villeroi remained convinced that he had nothing with which to reproach himself. He had been instructed by his King to go out and fight Marlborough, and had done so; he had been warned to pay particular attention to the deployment of the British troops, and had done so; he had done his best; when driven from the field of battle, he had then given ground regardless

William Billinge:
A Veteran of Ramillies

Inscription on a tombstone in Longnor, Staffordshire

IN MEMORY of William Billinge, who was born in a Cornfield at Fourfieldhead in this Parish in the Year 1679. At the age of 23 years he enlisted into His Majesty's Service under Sir George Rooke and was at the taking of the Fortress of Gibraltar in 1704. He afterwards served under the Duke of Marlborough at the ever Memorable Battle of Ramillies fought on 23rd May 1706 where he was wounded by a musket shot in the thigh. He afterwards returned to his native country and with Manly Courage defended his Sovereigns rights at the Rebellions in 1715 and 1745. He died within a space of 150 yards of where he was born and was interred here the 30 January 1791 aged 112 years.

BILLETED by Death I quartered here remain
When the trumpet sounds I rise and march again.

of the effect on his own reputation, to save what was left of his army for future operations – in his own eyes, a creditable thing. The one alternative to retreat after such a defeat was to fight another action, which, in the now enfeebled state of the French army, was plainly not advisable. Given all this, the Marshal saw no reason why he should not continue to enjoy the trust of his King and remain in command of the French army in the Low Countries. He appeared blind to the fact that no one any more had faith in his abilities; Louis XIV would spare his feelings as much as he could, but the Marshal had to be replaced as soon as possible – when, at last, it was found that Villeroi would not give up his command, it was given out by Versailles that he had asked to be replaced; so, in effect, he 'was resigned'.

The fortnight-long hectic pace of Marlborough's pursuit, impressive though it undoubtedly was, depended to a large degree on the logistical demands of his army. There was little, if any, formed body of French troops immediately in front of him to oppose his advance, although some rearguards were posted by Villeroi, and trees were felled, bridges broken down and meadows flooded in a game, but rather futile, attempt to slow the victorious advance of the Duke's armies. The pressing daily need to feed his troops, with supplies dragged along the bad roads of the time, exerted the only real brake on the Allied progress. Fortresses and towns submitted to his commanders – Alost, Oudenarde, Mechelin, Ghent, Bruges, Courtrai – in some cases with hardly a shot being fired. The Marquis de Vallée, the governor of Dendermonde, which controlled navigation of both the Dender river and the Scheldt, decided to put up a fight, however, and as a result, these vital waterways, so necessary in bringing forward guns, powder, food and materiel, were denied to the Allies for the time being. Marlborough, aware of the value of the place, wrote on 1 June to the States-General in The Hague: 'Dendermonde is under water, but I am endeavouring to make the Governor propositions that may tempt him to declare for King Charles.' It was a vain hope and the fortress stood firm for precious weeks. The Duke's summons to the governor to surrender the town on terms had met with a noticeably robust response from de Vallée that, 'The place being well garrisoned and provided with all necessaries for its defence, he hoped to merit his Grace's esteem, by discharging his duty and the trust reposed in him.'

News was now coming in to Marlborough that the contingents of Prussian, Hanoverian and Hessian troops, so long delayed for reasons which may have been good or bad, but whose lack on the day of battle might have had such serious consequences for the outcome, were pressing hastily forward to take a hand in the campaign. 'This', Marlborough wrote wearily, 'I take to be owing to our late success.' The reluctance of their rulers to commit the soldiers at the start of operations had understandably evaporated with the triumph at Ramillies, and all were now eager to participate and share whatever glory was to be had in the pursuit of the broken French and Bavarian army. In the meantime, Marlborough received reassurance on a matter that had been troubling him; his friend Sidney Godolphin wrote from London, 'You may depend that Her Majesty will not fail to take care of poor Bringfield's widow.'

The great port of Antwerp did not submit immediately, but the resistance of the garrison did not last for long. The governor, the Marquis de Tarazena, declared for King Charles III on 6 June, as did most of his own Walloon troops, and in this way seven of these excellent battalions of infantry joined Marlborough's army; the French soldiers in the garrison were permitted to march away without giving their parole. Veldt Marshal Overkirk then moved on to attack Ostend, with the assistance of a squadron of Royal Navy bomb-ketches whose bombardment soon set the town alight. On 4 July, the defences of Ostend, 'reduced to a heap of rubbish' by the bombardment, were stormed by a Dutch infantry battalion led by a forlorn hope of fifty British grenadiers. The seizure of the port provided Marlborough with a valuable direct route to the English Channel for communication and supply.

In the meantime, the Elector of Bavaria, having recovered his spirits a little, slipped some reinforcements into Dendermonde ('rushed [them] in soon after the place was blocked up'), elbowing aside a rather feeble attempt to prevent him, much to Marlborough's annoyance. The Duke wrote, 'The Elector of Bavaria has taken advantage of the siege of Ostend and the army's being there to cover it, to put a reinforcement of about four hundred foot and one hundred dragoons into Dendermonde.' He then added, not without a hint of gentle sarcasm, 'Brigadier Meredyth was upon his guard, but had not the strength to prevent it, he had five or six men killed, and as many, with a captain, taken prisoners.' The siege operations against the town were delayed, and an eight-day-long bombardment at the end of June failed to intimidate the Marquis de Vallée. The conditions were particularly difficult: troops to invest the town were in short supply, as was ammunition, and weather was particularly hot, so operations were reduced for the time being to a simple blockade. Dendermonde had particularly strong water defences, and Louis XIV scoffed that the Allied commanders had better use ducks if their siege was to be a success. Only when William Cadogan and Charles Churchill (the Duke's younger brother) went to take charge of the operations a few weeks later did the defences begin to fail.

The powerful Vauban-designed fortress of Menin, close to the border with France, had been invested by 23 July; the garrison comprised twelve battalions of infantry and three dismounted dragoon squadrons. On 5 August the lines of circumvallation and contravallation were complete, and the digging of trenches by Allied pioneers began the next day. Meanwhile, the Duc de Vendôme, one of Louis XIV's most bruising field commanders, had arrived from Italy, and began to scrape together a field army once more. The task was daunting, and Vendôme commented bitterly on the low state of morale amongst the troops, even those who had not been present at the catastrophe of Ramillies. He wrote to Michel de Chamillart from Valenciennes:

> With regard to the troops in the Spanish service, no one can answer for them; but that grieves me far less than the sadness and dejection that appears in the French army. I will do my best to restore their spirit, but it will be no light matter for me to do so, for everyone here is ready to take off his hat at the mere mention of the name of Marlborough.

By the second week of the month the Allied bombardment of Menin was well under way, but Vendôme moved suddenly forward on 15 August, with a substantial force scraped together from the garrisons in Lille and Tournai, to threaten Allied lines of communication and to disrupt Marlborough's foraging parties. Vendôme had no intention of being made to stand and fight a battle, but in the skirmishing that followed William Cadogan was taken prisoner by a French cavalry patrol, 'from whom we met with quarter and civility', the Allied Quartermaster General remembered ruefully, 'except their taking my watch and money.' Cadogan was released soon afterwards, to Marlborough's great relief, in exchange for Lieutenant General Pallavacini, a Savoyard officer in the service of France, who had been captured by the Allies earlier in the campaign. In a rather chivalrous touch, Vendôme (in many ways a somewhat uncouth man) speeded up the exchange, as he knew how much Marlborough valued Cadogan's services! A week after the covered way at Menin was stormed by the Allies, at heavy cost, the garrison commander, Count Caraman (veteran of the fight at Elixheim) capitulated, and was permitted to march away with his troops to Douai: 'With twelve battalions of Foot, and four squadrons of dragoons ... the besiegers found in the town fifty-five cannon of brass, ten of iron, six mortars and 810 double barrels of powder.'

With the arrival of Vendôme to take over what might have seemed to a less resourceful commander a perfectly poisoned chalice, Villeroi had been replaced as army commander in Flanders. His reputation was in ruins after Ramillies, of course, but Louis XIV was forgiving, greeting his old friend on return to Versailles with the kind words: 'At our age, Marshal, we must no longer expect good fortune', apparently a reference to their young days when the two men had gone philandering amongst the beauties at Court. Forgiven, but now quickly forgotten as a commander, Villeroi never led an army in the field again, a brave, honest soldier, who had the dire misfortune to meet in open battle an opponent so immeasurably his superior. His rather sad comment to the King was that he could now look forward to only one happy day, that of his own death.

Dendermonde held out well beyond the month of

August, and this very quickly became a real concern for Marlborough, exerting a stranglehold on the free use of the Scheldt and Dender rivers. The resistance by the garrison was a very creditable achievement as the Allied operations were helped by the unusually dry weather which depleted the otherwise formidable water-defences of the place. A British officer remembered, 'Old men up to seventy years observe they never saw such a drought, or the waters so low about the town.' The Allied trenches were opened on 1 September, and the Marquis de Vallée submitted six days later; within twenty-four hours heavy rain began to fall, completely flooding the Allied trenches and making them uninhabitable. The waterways were at last open to use by Allied resupply barges, and the French grip on these vital arteries of war was prised loose, at last, and not a moment too soon.

By 9 September Marlborough was shifting his attention from Dendermonde to lay siege to the town of Ath, 'a strong fortress', as Donald McBane, a noted Scottish swordsman serving with Orkney's regiment, remembered. The siege artillery came up the Scheldt to Oudenarde and on 16 September the place was invested by Overkirk with his Dutch corps. The trenches before Ath were opened on 20 September, and a lodgement made on the covered way a week or so later, after a well-executed counterattack by the garrison was beaten back on 27 September. The garrison surrendered on 2 October, rather than face a storm, and went as prisoners of war to Holland, 2,000 soldiers in all, to await exchange. Meanwhile, news came in to the Allied camp, courtesy of a message sent over by the French, of Prince Eugene's stunning victory at Turin earlier in the month, which saved Savoy for the Grand Alliance and killed the French commander, Marshal Ferdinand Marsin, in the process. Marlborough immediately wrote with the news to London: 'I think it my duty to give the Queen the earliest account I could of it.'

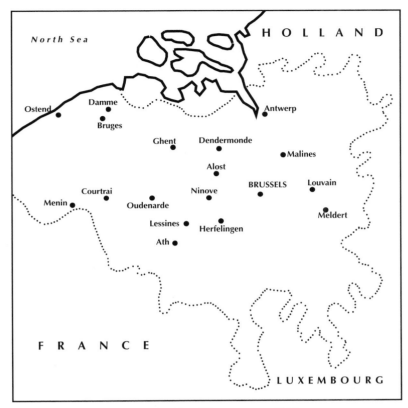

Marlborough's conquests after Ramillies, summer 1706.

With the arrival of the first week in October 1706, the Dutch were looking forward to their winter quarters; much had been attempted and much achieved, and they had played a major part in the successes of the year. Still, Marlborough wanted one more effort, despite concerns at the heavy rain which turned the roads to quagmires and marooned the big guns of the siege train; he planned to seize the important fortresses of Charleroi and Mons, lying close to the French border. For all his urging, the Dutch deputies refused to do more, and Marlborough, after reviewing his victorious regiments, sent them off to their quarters, Veldt Marshal Overkirk remaining in command in the Southern Netherlands. Mons would eventually fall to the Allied army in the damp autumn of 1709, but only after the bitterly fought battle in the woods at Malplaquet, where the Dutch infantry, as it turned out, were to pay a bloody price in a French artillery ambush for the opportunity to go on and lay siege to the town. Mons fell soon after that battle, but the cost had been very high, when the place could have been had at a cheap price three years earlier.

The autumn of 1706 sped onwards, and the astonishing year drew to a close; Marlborough could reflect with pride and perfect justice on his achievement. The French had not been expected to fight at all that year, and a dismal prospect loomed ahead as the Duke took the campaign trail. To general surprise, Villeroi came out to fight, and his army was shattered in one short afternoon. With his military strength broken, the French commander had then chosen, quite rightly, to save what was left of his army, and abandoned the Spanish Netherlands almost entirely. Those garrisons that he left behind put up, in the main, a feeble resistance. Louis XIV would rebuild his military strength along the northern border of France, but this took time, as regiments and generals were summoned from distant theatres of war, surrendering hard-won gains elsewhere, to hold the line. In the meanwhile, the initiative in the war, especially now that Prince Eugene had saved Turin, lay firmly with the Grand Alliance. 'Here', Richard Kane wrote, 'ends the Glorious Campaign of 1706.'

Increasingly, Louis XIV looked for ways to get out of what was fast becoming a ruinous war for France, unaware that the Grand Alliance had neither the wit nor the will to conclude a peace on terms that would satisfy both claimants to the throne in Madrid. With French military power broken in the Spanish Netherlands (at least for the time being), and the King's prestige severely damaged in the aftermath of the disaster at Ramillies and defeat at Turin, a peace tolerable if not actually advantageous to all sides was

Contemporary playing card, depicting the poor condition of France after the defeat at Ramillies.

a possibility. It was not to be: the heady successes in the year raised expectations throughout the Grand Alliance, which became greedy; the utter defeat of France, unimaginable in other circumstances, seemed now to be available, and so the war went on.

Once again, in 1707 as in 1705, Marlborough would find campaigning in the Southern Netherlands a frustrating business, not just on account of the old problem of the Dutch and their, understandable, caution, but because the Duc de Vendôme would prove to be a cunning and astute opponent, able to lead the Duke on and then turn away adroitly at the last moment and avoid the clash of arms which might settle things. Early in the summer of 1708, however, Vendôme at last overreached himself; although neatly stealing the important towns of Ghent and Bruges from under Marlborough's nose, he then allowed his army to be surprised and mauled by the Duke beside the Scheldt river at the Battle of Oudenarde in July. Within six months Marlborough had gone on to invade France and capture Lille, France's second city; Louis XIV would end that year of awful defeats by suing for peace with the Allies on almost whatever terms he could obtain.

Chapter 7

WALKING RAMILLIES BATTLEFIELD: A GUIDE

RAMILLIES BATTLEFIELD IS REALLY TOO FAR for the visitor from the UK to get to comfortably and then return home in a single day. When driving straight to the battlefield from the Channel Tunnel or ferry, the journey by car is a good two to three hours, depending on the traffic. It can all be done in a day, of course, as the author can testify, but insufficient time is then available to explore the field and do it justice. So, the visitor should allow two days – time that will be well rewarded on this wonderful site. The most convenient route is that past Tournai and Lille (both the scene of major Marlburian sieges), and on to the Brussels area.

A good place to use as a base for a Ramillies visit is, strangely enough, Waterloo, just to the south of Brussels. By doing so, the battlefield visitor has a variety of decent hotels to choose from. In the spirit of 'killing two birds with one stone' the site of Wellington's famous victory can also be taken in, as well as enjoying the more unspoilt pleasures of Ramillies, which is only about half an hour's drive to the south and east.

There is little opportunity in Ramillies or neighbouring villages for the visitor to get refreshments, but the small town of Egheze only five minutes' drive to the south has a good selection of bars and cafes – the Cheval Blanc is the author's favourite hostelry for friendly and prompt service at lunchtime. Belgian weather being what it is, a visit between the months of May and September is likely to be most promising. May is particularly good of course as, if the visit is timed well, the anniversary of the battle on the 23rd of that month can be celebrated on the field itself.

In addition to Ramillies, the visitor might also like to seek out the Williamite battlefield of Landen, and Marlborough's 1705 triumph at Elixheim, both of which (only a few hundred metres apart) are just a few miles to the north, alongside the battlefield of Neerwinden (1793). The great fortress of Namur is about half an hour's drive to the south, and only slightly farther afield is Mons (1709/1914), with the Malplaquet (1709) battlefield, and that of Jemappes (1792) and Le Cateau (1914), nearby. It can fairly be said that the interested battlefield visitor has an embarrassment of riches from which to choose when visiting this fascinating area.

STANDING BESIDE THE CURIOUS tree-crowned hillock, or tumulus, known as the Tomb of Ottomonde, slightly to the rear of the mile and a half wide plain between the villages of Ramillies and Taviers, the visitor to this beautiful spot is treated to one of the great battlefield vistas in the world, hardly changed across the 300 years since the event. The field, when looked at across the intervening slightly undulating land around the tomb itself towards the vast expanse of cornfield, can be seen to be very flat, although gently rising to the north. On this marvellous wide stage, the important watershed feature between the Mehaigne and Petite Gheete streams, a great cavalry battle was fought, on Whit Sunday, 23 May 1706, perhaps involving 25,000 horsemen. That battle was dramatically lost by the French cavalry commanders, leading immediately to the collapse of Marshal Villeroi's army, and the loss of Belgium.

The view from the foot of the tomb is deceptive, though, for the more broken terrain beyond Ramillies village to the north is completely hidden from sight; it is in dead ground, that oh so dangerous space which should concern all commanders when choosing a spot from which to fight. In that dead ground, leading along the valley of the Petite Gheete stream and its minor tributaries towards Offuz (Offus in modern usage) and Autre-Eglise, the Duke of Marlborough chose to throw in his main infantry effort early on in the battle, and by doing so, induced his less alert opponent to send vital troop reserves northwards, away from the support of the French cavalry in the crucial battle on the wide plain. This cavalry was the centre of gravity of the French and Bavarian army, and it became exposed to the Duke's schemes. At the masterful height of his tactical powers, Marlborough then adroitly switched his own main effort from the north to the south and commenced the ruthless destruction of the French squadrons from their weakened and glaringly exposed right flank.

It is pleasant to be able to say, in the 300th anniversary year of this huge conflict, that the Ramillies battlefield is still unencumbered with lion mounds, gift shops, ye-olde tea rooms, car-parks, regimental memorials, sign-post markers, tourist trails and interpretative boards, and all the assorted modern debris that litters and spoils so many other sites. A small number of the now inevitable modern wind-farm type windmills on the far horizon do not impinge on the scene very much. The villages of Taviers and Franquenée (formerly Franquenay) in the south, and Ramillies, Offus and Autre-Eglise, lying just to the north of the watershed between the Mehaigne and Petite Gheete, are, as can be expected, larger and more prosperous than would have been the case in the early eighteenth century. Also, although the countryside is generally quite open and rolling, the scattered copses and woods are probably rather more numerous these days. The villages still retain their individual characters, however, and many of the cottages and farms date back to that time; the interested visitor can get a very good idea of the atmosphere of the area, as it might have been in 1706, without too great an effort of imagination. Noticeably, in the south, the vast 'big-sky and big-horizon' expanse of the plain between Ramillies and Taviers has an air of quiet grandeur, while the more broken country to the north of Ramillies has a rather more closed-in, almost constricted, feel, well suited to the visitor who wishes to envisage the brutal infantry battles that raged in the smoke and flame for possession of the villages there.

The lie of the land of the Ramilles battlefield is not particularly complex, but there are some deceptive twists and hidden corners, and so a few moments' study of the map is recommended, before the tour proper commences, with compass in hand (Institut National Géographique, No. 40, Wavre, 1:50,000 scale – obtainable from Stanford Map Supplies in Covent Garden). This time and effort by the new visitor to the field is well repaid. The only reason that the armies of Marshal Villeroi and the Duke of Marlborough fought here at all was that the passage from east to west, or vice versa, in this region was made difficult, if not actually impossible, by the many small, marshy rivers and streams there. The 2,000-metre-wide plain between the headwaters of the Petite Gheete around Ramillies and the bogs of the Mehaigne at Taviers to the south, offered that firm ground and easy route so valuable to, and eagerly sought after by, army commanders. The eminent British military historian, Sir John Fortescue, described the ground:

> From the stream [the Mehaigne] the ground rises northwards in a steady wave for about half a mile, sinks gradually and [then] rises into a higher wave at Ramillies, sinks once more to the northwards of that village and rolls downward in a gentler undulation to Autre-Eglise.

So the southern part of the battlefield is well-drained ground, firm underfoot and ideal for horses and the passage of guns and wagons, an asset not easily found elsewhere in the region. Both the French Marshal and the English Duke knew this; they had each scouted the whole area the previous year, during the campaign that led to the forcing of the Lines of Brabant. This knowledge, inevitably it might seem, led them both to Ramillies that Sunday in May; that was how they came to fight there.

Looking at the topography from the map, it can be seen that the battlefield of Ramillies is situated at the highest point on the plains of Brabant. The fall in the ground towards the streams in the area, to both north and south, is quite pronounced, albeit gently shelving in places (particularly on the open ground to the south of that village, which is, in effect, a plateau between the headwaters of the Petite Gheete and the Mehaigne) – hence the existence of the important geographical watershed feature. The 'high' ground around Ramillies village is at about 150 to 155 metres above sea level, while the ground to the east, the area of the plateau of Jandrenouille from which the Allied army marched to battle is only, on average, slightly less, with just one elevated place, in particular, to site guns. The ground to the west, on the plateau of Mont St André, is undulating and rather higher in many places. So the expression 'ridge-line' which is often applied to accounts of the battle (including in this book) when describing the terrain between Ramillies, Offus and Autre-Eglise to the north can be a little misleading. It only ranks as such (and quite a modest feature it is, at best) by being made steep to the visitor who has to descend on foot into the valley of the Petite Gheete stream when approaching those villages from

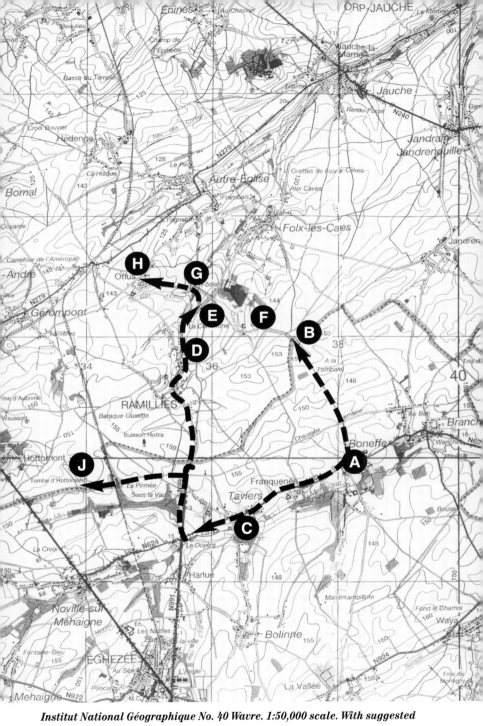

Institut National Géographique No. 40 Wavre. 1:50,000 scale. With suggested tour itinerary.

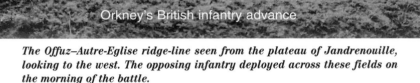

De la Guiche's Walloon infantry

Orkney's British infantry advance

The Offuz–Autre-Eglise ridge-line seen from the plateau of Jandrenouille,
looking to the west. The opposing infantry deployed across these fields on
the morning of the battle.

the east, as the Allied infantry had to do from where they had
formed up on the edge of the plateau of Jandrenouille. In fact,
the valley of the Petite Gheete stream in the north falls away to
less than 120 metres below Autre-Eglise, while the Mehaigne at
Taviers in the south is about 140 metres above sea level.

A GOOD STARTING PLACE for the visitor, whether on foot or
by vehicle, to the Ramillies battlefield, is at the small hamlet of
Boneffe on the N264 road (Point A on the adjoining map) just to
the east of the plain on which the great cavalry battle was
fought. Apart from the fact that Colonel Wertmüller and his
brigade of Dutch Guards formed up and stepped off from here
in the opening clash of the afternoon, by looking to the north and
the east, it is possible to get a good idea of the wide extent of
the plateau of Jandrenouille to the north, across which the Allied
army came on its approach to battle. Open and fairly level,
devoid of any major natural obstacle, this afforded an excellent
forming up area for the Duke of Marlborough when making his
arrangements, the troops shaking out rapidly from line of march
to column of attack, in response to his urgent messages. The
speed with which the Duke could do this left the French

commander with little chance to change his mind and draw off and avoid battle (although, in fact, he showed no sign of actually wishing to do so). A couple of miles to the east, just out of sight, the Allied troops marched over the demolished Lines of Brabant (no sign of these defences today, of course), and the ghostly Williamite battlefield of Landen is a little to the north, beyond which the soldiers would have remembered the fight at Elixheim the previous year.

Going from Boneffe along the path in a northerly direction, within a few hundred metres the track known as the Chausée Romaine (Roman road) is reached, crossing from west to east. The church spire in Ramillies village can be clearly made out to the westwards (care is needed as Taviers, Ramillies, Offus and Autre-Eglise church spires and towers can all be seen at varying points, and a compass is very handy to maintain true direction-finding on the wide open plain). A glance to the left, back towards the N624 road will show the small hamlets of Franquenée and Taviers, where the Swiss and the Dutch fought such a desperate battle for possession – 'almost as bloody as the rest of the battle put together', it was remembered. Going onwards onto the plateau of Jandrenouille to the 153-metre elevation feature (Point B), the visitor gets a good view to the west of the Ramillies–Offus ridge-line, occupied by Villeroi's army. In this immediate area, making use of the relatively high ground on the otherwise gently rolling plateau, Marlborough established his great battery of 24-pounder guns with which to engage the French artillery in and around Ramillies.

By retracing the route to Boneffe, and going westwards along the N624, Franquenée is soon reached. The hamlet is still separated from Taviers by the marshy water-meadows of the Mehaigne river and its tributary the Visoule stream (which rises near to the Tomb of Ottomonde), although these are largely drained now, but the reedy grass, the damp ground underfoot and a few willow trees give the game away. Go on to Taviers itself, pausing to consider the desperate battle at bayonet point that the Dutch Guards won there. Looking to the north (from Point C) towards Ramillies, it can be seen that artillery placed there could not support the Swiss garrison in Taviers, and vice versa, although, if sited properly, a cross-fire of a kind might have been achieved to hamper the Allied cavalry as it advanced onto the plain to give battle. In the event, with their lack of numbers in the opening exchanges and only a botched counterattack to help them, the Swiss had little chance of holding the place. The determined attack put in by Wertmüller's Dutch veterans, backed up by light artillery, completely unhinged the right of the French line of battle at the very outset of the fighting, and they never really recovered their poise.

The visitor should then go from Taviers along to the crossroads junction of the N264 and the N991, turning to the north along the N991 towards the village of Ramillies itself. Within a few hundred metres the old Roman road (Chausée Romaine) is crossed, going from west to east. On the left is the wide rolling plain, now still laid to arable crops as in 1706, over which de Guiscard's French cavalry were deployed to meet Overkirk's Dutch and Württemberg's Danish squadrons. It is so obviously perfect country for mounted action, a great open arena on which the commanders on both sides could exercise their troopers' skill to the utmost. The ground rises very gently from 148 metres above sea level to 155 metres on the plateau between the area around Ottomonde and Ramillies. Despite their lack of numbers, and the lack of proper infantry support, de Guiscard's cavalry put in a fine performance, and it took a hard struggle before the Danes could slip past their right flank to the hill known as the Tomb of Ottomonde (seen with its crown of trees, quite distinctly, in the distance) and turn to face the raw open flank of the, by then, off-balance French and Bavarian army.

Going further northwards along the N991 (passing the Chemin de Marlborough on the way, on the edge of the village) the visitor soon comes to the centre of Ramillies itself. Alessandro Maffei's headquarters, La Haute Censée (where the barn still shows signs of musket-shot from the battle – see illustration on p. 94) is passed on the left-hand side, and soon afterwards, on the right of the road, is the church (Point D). This is a rather plain building with a churchyard littered with some decrepit First World War relics. There is no obvious sign now of the field of rye in which the Scots and the French fought with such ferocity in 1706, and where Ensign James Gardner was shot and left for dead alongside the churchyard wall, after losing the regimental colour (before being aided by two French soldiers who took pity on him). The walled graveyard now sits there, and it is a good spot from which to consider the disposition of the French and Bavarian armies and the arrangements they made for the defence of Ramillies, and to see the view that Villeroi's commanders had of the Allied army as it came on in the morning sunshine across the plateau of Jandrenouille. It will be noticed from this spot, by reference to the map, that Autre-Eglise to the north (the left of Villeroi's line of battle) and Taviers to the south (the right of his line) both curl around the observer; the French line was an enormous arched formation, inconvenient for moving troops quickly from one flank to another.

The houses in Ramillies village itself are, not surprisingly, larger and more prosperous than the mean cottages of the early eighteenth century would have been, but the general feel of the place makes it easy to imagine the desperate infantry struggle as the Allied infantry tried, and failed several times, to break their way in, being repulsed on each occasion by the valiant French garrison, aided by their Irish and German allies. Almost opposite the church is a lane that leads up towards Offus and the plateau of Mont St André, and here Maffei made his stand with the German brigade, before being taken prisoner by the Dutch cavalry.

Just on the northern edge of Ramillies there is a slight crest where the N991 road bends to the right (Point E). The plateau of Jandrenouille is on the right, and standing on that verge and gazing to the westwards, the visitor is looking across the valley of the Petite Gheete stream itself, towards Offus – the church spire is plainly to be seen ahead – and the plateau of Mont St André. Looking slightly to the north it is just possible also to see amongst the trees the tower (not a spire, unlike its neighbours) of the church in Autre-Eglise at the very left end of Villeroi's line of battle. That is the area where the Elector of Bavaria massed his cavalry and infantry, and to which the French Marshal hurried his vital reserves in response to the growing, but illusory, threat to his flank, to the dire detriment of the conduct of the cavalry battle on his right.

Before leaving the viewing point on the edge of the plateau of Jandrenouille, by looking to the east, it is possible to make out the slight re-entrant, partly screened by trees, formed by headwaters of the small La Quivelette stream which flows away

Offuz church spire, seen from the south.

to the north and its confluence with the Petite Gheete near Autre-Eglise. This small fold in the ground leading across the plateau to the south, a very slight depression to the casual observer, was enough to hide from the view of Villeroi and his officers Marlborough's reinforcement of his strength in the centre and the south of the battlefield, as he subtly shifted the weight of his attack from his right to the left. The farm by the stream (Point F) is reputedly the place where the Duke of Marlborough established his headquarters, although he spent most of the day on horseback supervising his commanders.

By walking down the gentle slope into the valley on the other side of the N991 road, leading down towards Fodia and the Petite Gheete itself, the visitor is following the route taken by Thomas Kitcher and his comrades in the British infantry battalions as they drove de la Guiche's brigade of Walloon infantry away from the marshy stream (now a culverted

The Petite Gheete valley, seen from Offuz. The opposing infantry are indicated.

Orkney's attack on Offuz village

Walloon defenders

Looking northwards across the plateau of Jandrenouille to the re-entrant formed by La Quivelette stream. Marlborough used this shallow feature to conceal his movement of troops towards the attack on Ramillies from Villeroi.

watercourse lined with trees and with little obvious sign remaining of the marshes through which the Allied troops had to wade). A glance at the map will show that the valley drops quite markedly from 143 metres to about 125 metres in elevation in the space of only about 400 metres walked (Point G). So the Petite Gheete stream valley, especially in the marshy conditions of the early eighteenth century, presented quite an obstacle, to infantry as well as their mounted comrades nearby. The Walloons made the most of this advantage; Tom Kitcher noted that the British cavalry and dragoons appeared to hang back in the opening attacks, and it is easy to see why, although they managed the passage of the stream in the end.

Leaving Fodia and walking up the lane leading towards Offus village, within a few hundred metres the visitor arrives at a walled farmyard (typical of the region) on the edge of that village (Point H). Here, beside the farmhouse, it is possible to get a good view back across the Petite Gheete valley towards the Allied lines, taking in the view that so fascinated the French commander and the Elector of Bavaria when they should have been attending to their increasingly fragile right flank. This is the

135

Walled farm on the edge of Offuz village.

The valley of the Petite Gheete stream. The advance of Orkney's British infantry is indicated.

The British infantry advance into Petite Gheete valley

ground held with such tenacity by the Walloon and French infantry under de la Guiche, in the face of the ferocious British infantry attacks sent in by Earl Orkney, who eventually managed to force his way into Offus itself. Had he gone on, and not heeded Marlborough's imperative command to return to the edge of the plateau of Jandrenouille, the Earl would have been unsupported and attacked by the Elector of Bavaria's cavalry, massed on the ridge-line leading to Autre-Eglise in the north and the area behind Ramillies to the south, which follows the general route of the modern N239 road.

At the end of the tour, it is well worth going back southwards through Ramillies village, along the N991 to the Chausée Romaine. Turn right and go along the track across the plain to the Tomb of Ottomonde (Point J). It is probably not worth the effort to climb up on to the feature, as the many trees on the summit severely impede the view. However, the view from the base over the adjacent fields is terrific, looking north and east across an intervening shallow depression towards the scene of

The Elector of Bavaria's cavalry

Lumley's British cavalry and dragoons

The ridge-line near Autre-Eglise where Henry Lumley's British cavalry charged and broke the Elector of Bavaria's cavalry, and destroyed the Régiment du Roi.

the cavalry battle, where de Guiscard's valiant troopers all afternoon fought their desperate, doomed, action against the overwhelming Dutch and Danish squadrons of Overkirk and Württemberg. Away across those fields can be seen the cottages of Ramillies, with the church spire of Offus just discernible beyond. There Marlborough's subtle but devastating deceit was played on his opponent, obliging the French commander to reinforce those secondary operations in the north, at the very moment that the more vital sector, on the very edge of which the fortunate present-day visitor now stands, came under most critical threat.

The plain to the south of Ramillies where the Danish cavalry swept around the right flank of Villeroi's army.

BIBLIOGRAPHY

It seems strange that no single individual written work has been devoted to such a significant event as the Battle of Ramillies. Few battles were as sudden and exciting, or victory more complete and astonishing, while such profound and lasting effects on European history would seem to have merited at least one book before now. Perhaps the events on the Sunday in May were so stark, so stunning in their impact, the success so incontrovertible, that there was not much more to say, beyond stating the bald facts. Well, that is not the case – there is plenty to ponder over when considering the catastrophe that overtook Marshal Villeroi's fine army, and eminent authors such as Frank Taylor, Winston Churchill and David Chandler have in their own ways devoted extensive chapters to the battle in their published works, which are listed below.

All battles have within their complex details some small mysteries, and Ramillies is no exception, even leaving aside the rather large mystery of why it took Villeroi so long to realize what Marlborough was up to (the lie of the ground doesn't entirely explain it). There is considerable, well-documented, comment on the timely arrival of the Danish cavalry who took such a prominent part in the destruction of the French right Wing. However, rather less is known, or commented on, about the Danish infantry who also took part in the fighting that day. That they did so is not in doubt, for they provided the depth battalions during Orkney's attack on Offuz and Autre-Eglise, but their presence with the Duke's army, when their mounted compatriots were, until a very late stage, absent and waiting for their arrears of pay, is a puzzle. The foot soldiers could hardly have kept pace with their mounted comrades on the march to join the Duke's army. However, John Millner in his *Compendious*

Journal (pp. 171 and 177), who took part in the fighting that day on the right flank, refers to the 'Danes Foot' and says that they 'join'd and fell in with six battalions and three squadrons of Danes more than the first number before given [Württemberg's twenty-one squadrons of cavalry].' Major Peter Verney's voluminous notes on the orders of battle of the armies also refer to the Danish infantry being in action, as does David Chandler in one of his footnotes to the John Deane memoirs (p. 33), so it seems that there was a second, later, reinforcement by the Danes, not usually mentioned in accounts of the campaign.

Prominent amongst the handful of available eye-witness accounts of the Ramillies battle is that left by Colonel Jean-Martin De La Colonie, whose erudite and informative memoirs were translated into English by W C Horsley and published in 1904 as the *Chronicles of an Old Campaigner.* Although this valiant French soldier was mostly engaged in the heavy fighting at the southern end of the Ramillies battlefield (without a great deal of success), his reminiscences of the events that rapidly overtook, and overwhelmed, the French and Bavarian armies that Sunday are vivid, interesting and valuable.

Alison, A, *Life of John, Duke of Marlborough*, 1852

Atkinson, C T, *Marlborough and the Rise of the British Army*, 1921

——, *Ramillies Battlefield, Journal of the Society for Army Historical Research (JSAHR)*, 1960

Barnett, C, *Marlborough*, 1974

Belloc, H, *The Strategy and Tactics of the Great Duke of Marlborough*, 1933

Bishop, M, *Life and Adventures, 1701–1711*, 1744

Burn, W, *A Scots Fusilier and Dragoon Under Marlborough*, *JSAHR*, 1936

Burrell, S (ed), *Amiable Renegade: Memoirs of Captain Peter Drake*, 1960

Burton, I, *The Captain General*, 1968

Chandler, D, *The Art of Warfare in the Age of Marlborough*, 1983

——, *Marlborough as Military Commander*, 1984

—— (ed), *Journal of John Deane, JSAHR*, 1984

—— (ed), *Captain Robert Parker and the Comte de Merode-Westerloo*, 1968

Churchill, W S, *Marlborough: His Life and Times*, 1947

Coxe, W, *Memoirs of John, 1st Duke of Marlborough*, 1848

Crockatt, J, *Marlborough*, 1971

Dickson, P, *Red John of the Battles*, 1973

Drake, P, *Memoirs*, 1755

Falkner, J, *Great and Glorious Days*, 2002

——, *Blenheim, 1704*, 2004

——, *Marlborough's Wars: Eye Witness Accounts*, 2005

Fortescue, J, *History of the British Army*, 1901

—— (ed), *Life and Adventures of Mrs Christian Davies*, 1929

Horsley, W (ed), *Chronicles of an Old Campaigner*, 1904

Kane, R, *Campaigns of King William and Queen Anne*, 1745

Lediard, T, *Life of John, Duke of Marlborough*, 1736

Liddell Hart Centre, *Papers of Major Peter Verney* (relating to Orders of Battle at Ramillies)

Millner, J, *A Compendious Journal*, 1733

Murray, G (ed), *Letters and Dispatches of the Duke of Marlborough*, 1845

Orkney (Hamilton), G, *Letters of 1st Earl Orkney, English Historical Review*, 1904

Parker, R, *Memoirs*, 1747

St John, B (ed), *Memoirs of the Duc de St Simon*, 1878

Taylor, F, *The Wars of Marlborough*, 1921

Tindal, N, *Continuation of Rapin's History of England*, 1738

Trevelyan, G, *Ramillies and the Union with Scotland*, 1932

Wykes, A, *The Royal Hampshire Regiment*, 1968

INDEX

Alègre, Yves, Marquis d', 6, 24–5, 35

Antwerp, 117

Argyll, John Campbell, 2nd Duke, 6, 75–7, 94

Ath, 120

Autre-Eglise, 42, 49, 54, 127; under attack by Orkney, 67–72, 85

Barrier Towns, 16

Billinge, William, 114

Blackader, Major John, 69–70

Bringfield, Lieutenant Colonel James, 6, 85–6, 108, 117

Brussels, capitulates to Marlborough, 109–10

Cadogan, Lieutenant General William, 6, 45; encounters French army at Ramillies, 44–6; sent to recall Orkney, 72, 118; taken prisoner outside Menin, 119

Calcinato, 33, 98

Campbell, James, 102

Campbell, John (see Argyll)

Caraman, Pierre-Paul, Count, 24–6; governor of Menin, 119

Carlos II, King of Spain, 15 casualties at Ramillies, 104–5

Chamillart, Michel de, 111–12, 114, 118

Churchill, General Charles, 6, 75, 118

Davies, Mrs Christian, wounded outside Ramillies, 99

Deane, John, 41, 85, 98, 140

De La Colonie, Colonel Jean-Martin, 6, 62, 74, 78–9, 104; optimism at forthcoming campaign, 31, 45–6;

counterattack on Taviers, 62–3; rallies his troops, 64–5; *Memoirs*, 50, 62, 140

de la Guiche, Major General, 68–9, 86, 89, 91, 137

de la Motte, General, 62

Dendermonde, 114, 116–17, 119–20

de Nonan, Brigadier General, 61

de Vallée, Marquis, defends Dendermonde, 116–17, 119–20

Dopff, General Daniel, 46

Drake, Peter, 44–6, 91, 98, 107

Dyle river, 26–8, 37, 48, 58, 102

Elixheim, 21; battle at, 21–6, 31, 50, 131

Eugene, Prince François (Eugene), of Savoy, 11, 33, 120, 122

Feuquières, Marquis de, 51, 80, 87–8, 98

Fodia, 134–5

Franquenay, 59, 127, 131

Gardiner, James, 77, 132–3

Goslinga, Sicco van, Dutch field deputy, 46, 49, 102, 110

Grimaldi, Honoré, Marquis de, 28–9

Guiscard, General (Marquis de), French cavalry commander, 50, 57, 59, 80–2, 87, 90, 112, 132, 138; troops are over-extended, 63–4, 66, 73

Haute Censée farm, 93–5, 132

Hay, Colonel John, Lord, 6, 25, 98

Huy, 13, 20, 31

Kane, Richard, 58, 66, 72, 81, 89,

92, 122
Kitcher, Thomas, 68–9, 135

La Quivelette stream, 133-4, 135
Liége, 20
Lines of Brabant, 22–6, 49, 131
Louis XIV of France, 10, 15–16, 19; strategic dilemma after Blenheim, 18–19, 26, 30–2; urges Villeroi to fight Marlborough, 34–5; advice to Villeroi, 58; receives news of the defeat, 111; removes Villeroi from command, 115; receives Villeroi at Versailles, 119
Louvain, 10, 28, 58; abandoned by Villeroi, 104; taken by Marlborough, 108
Lumley, Lieutenant General Henry, 6, 99, 102

McBane, Donald, 120
Maffei, Alessandro, Marquis de, 7, 75, 93–5, 132,133
Maison du Roi cavalry, 9, 32, 50, 53, 74, 79, 80–2; charge Marlborough, 82; begin to tire, 87–9; break ranks, 92–3, 98–9; Louis XIV's opinion of performance, 112
Malplaquet, 122, 126
Marlborough, John Churchill, 1st Duke, 9, 13; attempts Moselle valley campaign, 19–20; at Elixheim battle, 21–6; learns of Villeroi's advance, 37; concentrates his army, 37–9; closes up to French, 46–8; dispositions at Ramillies, 49–50; begins to shift weight of attack to the right, 78, 126–7; thrown from his horse, 82–5; sleeps on the ground, 102; despatch after the victory

108–9; captures Brussels, 110
Marsin, Ferdinand, Marshal, 18, 33–4; killed at Turin, 120
Mehaigne stream, 13, 24, 57, 63–5, 126
Menin, 10, 118
Millner, John, 63, 105, 139–40
Molesworth, Captain Robert, 83, 85
Mons, 121–2
Moselle valley, 19–20, 31, 37
Murray, Lieutenant General Robert, 7, 83–5

Namur, 21, 35–6
Neerysche, 28
Noyelles, Count, 23–4

O'Brien, Charles, 5th Viscount Clare, 7, 75, 94
Offuz, 14, 42, 74–5, 85, 126
Orkney, George Hamilton, 1st Earl, 7, 23, 25–6, 71; leads infantry into attack, 66–7; action at Petite Gheete valley, 77, 85, 89, 98, 137
Ostend, 117
Ottomonde, Tomb of, 90–2, 126
Oudenarde, 10; submits to Marlborough, 113, 114, 116; Battle of (1708), 124
Overkirk, Henry of Nassau, Count, 7, 20–1, 40; reluctant to pursue after Elixheim 26–7; troops at Tongres, 35, 38; before Battle of Ramillies, 46; leads cavalry forward, 57, 78–81, 132; cavalry begin to tire and suffer casualties, 88–9, 90; treatment of prisoners, 107; attacks Ostend, 117; command in Southern Netherlands, 121

Pallandt, Brigadier General van, 72
Parker, Captain Robert, 51, 81

143

Petite Gheete stream, 11, 13, 21, 37, 48, 56, 70, 86, 95, 126, 134
Ramillies, significance as a battle, 10–11; importance of strategic position, 13–14, 36, 38; topography, 42, 52–3; village under attack, 75, 77, 82, 85; garrison contained and driven out, 89, 94–5; the battlefield today, 126, 128–30

Schulemberg, Matthias-Johan, Count, 7, 75
Schultz, Major General, 75, 77
Slangenberg, General, 26–7, 30
Soignes, 29–30
Spaar, Major General, 75, 77, 94
States-General of Holland, 29–30, 34, 42
Swiss Troops, defend Franquenay and Taviers, 59–61

Tarazena, Marquis de, 117
Taviers, 54, 57, 60–2, 66, 104, 126–7, 131
Tirlemont, 23, 26–7, 37

Vauban, Sebastien Le Prestre, Marshal, urges Louis XIV to occupy Barrier Towns, 16
Vendôme, Louis-Joseph de Bourbon, Duc de, 7, 25, 33, 84, 118–19, 124
Villars, Claud Louis Hector, Marshal, 19, 31, 33
Villeroi, François de Neufville, Marshal, 7, 9, 19, 23, 27, 28, 39; mistakenly believes has foiled Marlborough, 30–1; urged to fight Marlborough, 34–5; takes up position at Ramillies, 37–9, 42; dispositions of army, 49–50; neglects right flank 57–8; loses grip on the battle, 66; over-concerned with left flank, 73–4; receives urgent pleas for assistance, 88; sees collapse of right flank 91–3; evades capture by British cavalry, 99; abandons Louvain and Brussels, 106–7; after the battle, 111; removed from command, 115; returns to Versailles, 119
Visoule stream, 57, 63, 85

Wertmüller, Colonel, brigade attacks Franquenay and Taviers, 59–63, 88, 130, 132
Wittelsbach, Maximilien-Emmanuel, Elector of Bavaria, 7–8, 15, 18, 43–4; hurries to battle, 55; warning to Villeroi, 58; attempts to reorder troops, 91, 133; fugitive, 99; writes to Louis XIV, 106; reinforces Dendermonde, 117
Wood, Lieutenant General Cornelius, 98
Württemberg, Karl-Alexander, Duke, 8, 38; joins Marlborough, 41; action at Ramillies, 63, 88, 92, 132, 138, 140; action at Oudenarde, 114

Yssche river, 28–9